ARTS & CRAFTS INSPIRATIONS

by Robert & Bob Belke

POPULAR WOODWORKING BOOKS

CINCINNATI, OHIO

www.popularwoodworking.com

TABLE OF CONTENTS

INTRODUCTION

A BRIEF LOOK AT THE ARTS & CRAFTS MOVEMENT

The Arts & Crafts Movement originated in England in the second half of the nineteenth century. The movement attempted to emphasize the importance of hand craftsmanship over the dehumanizing, impersonal mass production by machine. William Morris, (1834–1896), is considered the father of the Arts & Crafts Movement. Morris was inspired by the writings of John Ruskin, (1818–1900), who was a great critic of design and art. Both men disliked the badly designed, machine produced products coming out of the English factories. They also felt that the factory workers were

being dehumanized by the industrial system. William Morris, who was the originator of the Morris chair, was a firm believer in the craftsman-designer concept. He married Jane Burden and commissioned his friend, Phillip Webb, to build them a house at Bexley Heath, England. Morris realized there was no furniture currently being built that was suitable to furnish the house. Webb designed and built several pieces of furniture, which Morris and his friends, Edward Burne-Jones, and Dante Rossetti, then decorated.

Morris founded a company that designed and fabricated furniture, stained glass, wallpaper, fabric rugs and tapestries. Everything was done by hand. They soon discovered that hand-crafted items were expensive to make. They never solved this problem. So, hand-crafted Arts & Crafts items were actually only available to the well-to-do class of customers.

Toward the 1870s, William Morris became disenchanted with an economic system that made his products so expensive. He stood for an art for all rather than for the wealthy few, and a production system based upon cooperation rather than competition. He also came to realize that machines were necessary for production. In 1890, Morris founded the Kelmscott Press, which printed books about works of art, aired his views on honest craftsmanship and the improvement of the worker's conditions. Morris' influence was pervasive, not only in England, but extending to the other side of

the "pond". A gentleman named C. R. Ashbee, (1863–1942), founded *The Guild of Handicraft* in 1888, which echoed Morris' earlier thoughts, of the cooperative efforts in the Arts & Crafts. Ashbee was considered to be one of the major links between the English Arts & Crafts Movement and the American craftsmen. He visited the United States a number of times; lecturing at Cornell University, in Buffalo, and in Chicago. He met Frank Lloyd Wright, Charles Sumner Greene, and Elbert Hubbard.

Several publications, guilds and exhibitions sprang up in England, and made their way to the United States Several American guilds were formed emphasizing Arts & Crafts furniture and design.

Notable American names in the Arts & Crafts movement were, Elbert Hubbard, William P. Price, Hawley McLanahan, Ralf Ratcliffe, and the Stickley brothers. Hubbard established *The Roycraft Community* in East Aurora, New York. Hubbard employed talented artisans and produced furniture and handcrafted items that embodied the Arts & Crafts philosophy of simplicity, function, and beauty. William P. Price and Hawley McLanahan established the *Rose Valley crafts community* in Moylan Pennsylvania. The Stickley brothers established furniture factories in the Syracuse, New York area.

Arguably the most important Arts & Crafts figure in America during that era was the craftsman/designer/entrepreneur Gustav Stickley, (1858-1942), whose furniture was popularly known as *Mission Oak*. Stickley was the eldest of five brothers, grew up in rural Wisconsin, and went to work for his father as an apprentice stonemason. By the age of twelve, he had become a journeyman stonemason. He grew to hate stone masonry, probably because of being forced to work with such heavy items so early in life. In the early 1870s the elder Stickley abandoned his family, and they were forced to move east to Brandt, Pennsylvania, to live with Mrs. Stickley's brother, Jacob Schlaeger, who owned a small chair making factory. Gustav assumed the responsibility of supporting his large family and went to work for his uncle, learning to make chairs. He stated that this was the period when he came to appreciate the beauty of wood for its natural color, texture, and grain. He continued his employment with the Brandt Chair Company until 1884. He and two of his brothers, Charles and Albert, moved to Binghamton, New York, and established a wholesale and retail business. In 1888, his two other brothers, Leopold and John George would join the firm.

They sold black-walnut furniture from Grand Rapids, Michigan, chairs from Brandt, Pennsylvania, and Shaker furniture. In 1886, the Stickley brothers added a chair factory to their Binghamton enterprise. Since he had very little money for machines, most of the woodworking was done by hand. Lathe work was done either by using a hand-powered lathe or a

broom maker's lathe.

During 1888 and 1889, Gustav broke away from his brothers and formed another furniture company in Binghamton, partnering with Elgin A. Simonds. This company lasted about three years and was an important association for Gustav, since Simonds was to become his partner when he established the *Craftsman Shops*, in Syracuse, New York, in 1898.

During 1892-1894, along with his other enterprises, Stickley was Director of Manufacturing Operations at the *Auburn State Prison*, located in Auburn, New York. In this position, using convict labor, he produced simple chairs for sale to the general public. It is said that he made the first electric chair, which is still in place at the prison.

During 1892-1894, Gustav Stickley made his first trip to Europe and became impressed with the *Arts & Crafts Movement*. He began to experiment with straight and strong construction techniques used in furniture making. He unintentionally created a new *American Arts & Crafts style*. For most of his pieces, he used quarter-sawn white oak. He felt the pale color of the wood needed to be softened and darkened to give the appearance of age. He experimented with various finishes, including ammonia fuming. (When white oak is exposed to ammonia fuming, it turns dark, imparting a unique look he used for his furniture.)

During 1901, Gustav Stickley, adopted the Flemish motto *Als Ik Kan*.

Roughly translated *as best I can*. He imprinted this and a medieval joiner's compass on his furniture.

In 1903, Stickley employed a gifted designer named Harvey Ellis, (1852–1904) after they met at an Arts & Crafts exhibition in Rochester, New York. Ellis was responsible for the addition of light and graceful touches to Stickley's straight, stocky styles. He broke up the horizontals by using an arch on table or chest aprons and added color by inserting inlays. Harvey Ellis died about seven months after joining Stickley. Today, those curves seen on Stickley's furniture are referred to as the *Harvey Ellis curves*.

Gustav Stickley's younger broth-

ers, Leopold and J. George Stickley, made furniture in Fayettville, New York. Their furniture was considered of secondary importance to that of their brother, Gustav. They advertised that the crafting of furniture was their only business, and, that the skins they acquired for upholstery were so fresh, that the goats from which the hides came, had recently grazed the fields of the Holy Land. They offered customized dimensions to suit the customer's preference. Like most Craftsman furniture, L.& J.G Stickley's mission furniture was made of fumed oak and usually had straight lines; emulating Gustav's furniture. They did produce furniture that was their own design.

Gustav Stickley was an entrepreneur who had his fingers in many pies. Besides publishing the *Craftsman* magazine, he was involved in architecture, custom designing, and the building of houses. In the early 1900s, he opened

furniture showrooms and publishing offices in New York City. He had Craftsman stores in Boston and Washington, D.C. and kept his original factory in Syracuse, New York. With the popularity of Craftsman furniture, he had many competitors, among which were his brothers, L.& J.G. Stickley, in Fayetteville, New York, and his brothers Charles and Albert, in Grand Rapids, Michigan.

In 1916, due to overextending himself, the beginning of World War I, and the general declining popularity of the Arts & Crafts Movement in the US, Gustav Stickley went bankrupt. He returned to Syracuse, New York, and engaged in several business ventures with his brothers Leopold, John George, and Albert.

After Gustav's bankruptcy, in 1916, Leopold and J.G. Stickley purchased Gustav's factory outside of Syracuse, New York, and continued to produce furniture under the name *Stickley Manufacturing Company, Inc*.

The firm is still in full operation in Fayetteville and Manlius, New York,

In 1974, the Stickley operations were purchased by the Audi family, but they still retain the name Stickley in the company title. They are best known for high-end cherry-wood reproductions of early-American colonial furniture, and Mission furniture. Probably because of its simple lines and designs, Mission furniture is enjoying a present day renaissance.

TOOLS YOU WILL NEED

No special woodworking tools are needed to build the furniture in this book. A table saw, mortiser (either an attachment on your drill press or a dedicated machine), band saw and a drill press will do the job.

Hand tools needed are some chisels, a mallet or hammer, a hand drill, hand saw (either a back saw or regular hand saw), a coping saw and some screwdrivers.

A few extras might include a jig saw, a set of Forstner bits, twist drills, etc.

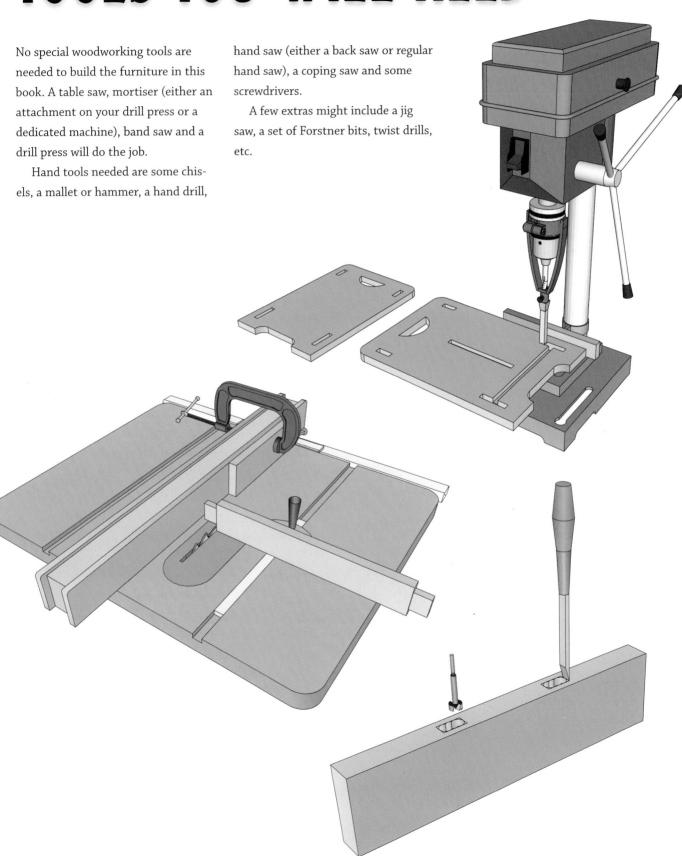

MISSION-STYLE MAGAZINE RACK

This magazine rack is designed in the Arts & Crafts, or Mission style. It features solid ends, stiles that are mortised in place and curved bottom rails, also called the Harvey-Ellis curve, named for the gentleman responsible for visually softening up most Mission furniture designs.

Placed beside an easy chair, this rack will comfortably hold all your favorite magazines. It's made from cherry wood and finished with satin polyurethane, and, will compliment any decor.

inches (millimeters)

REFERENCE	QUANTITY	PART	STOCK	THICKNESS	(mm)	WIDTH	(mm)	LENGTH	(mm)	COMMENTS
A	2	ends	hardwood	¾	(19)	12	(304)	7	(178)	
B	2	side top rails	hardwood	¾	(19)	2½	(64)	18	(457)	
C	2	side bottom rails	hardwood	¾	(19)	3½	(89)	18	(457)	
D	10	side stiles	hardwood	¾	(19)	2	(51)	10	(254)	
E	2	center rails	hardwood	¾	(19)	1½	(38)	15½	(394)	
F	2	center partitions	hardwood	¼	(6)	16¼	(413)	6¾	(171)	
G	2	bottoms	hardwood	¼	(6)	9¼	(235)	16	(406)	cut to fit

1 Two pieces of wood will most likely be needed to create each end. First, joint the edges to be joined, then glue up the pieces. Cut the ends to size, lay out the stopped grooves, the hand holds and the bottom cutouts.

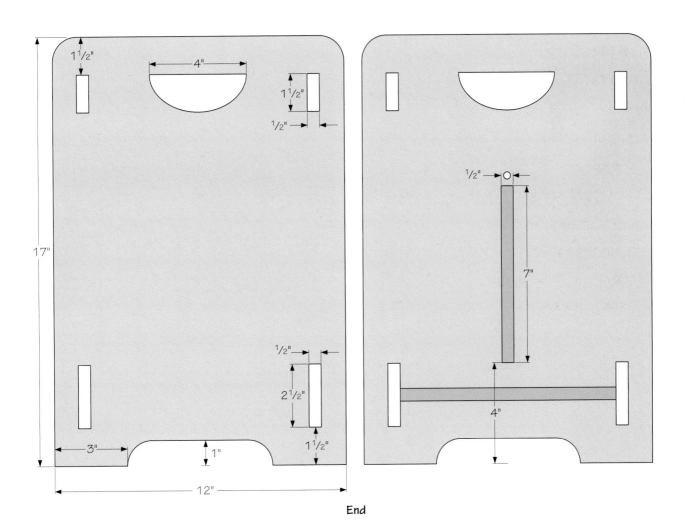

End

2 On the inside face of each end, lay out the dimension of the stopped grooves and dadoes. Using a mortiser, cut the eight through mortises. Bore a couple of pilot holes in the middle of the hand-hold layout with a ³⁄₄"-Forstner bit, then cut out the hand holds. The stopped dadoes can be routed using a ¹⁄₄"-router bit. Rout the dado wide enough to fit the center plywood panel.

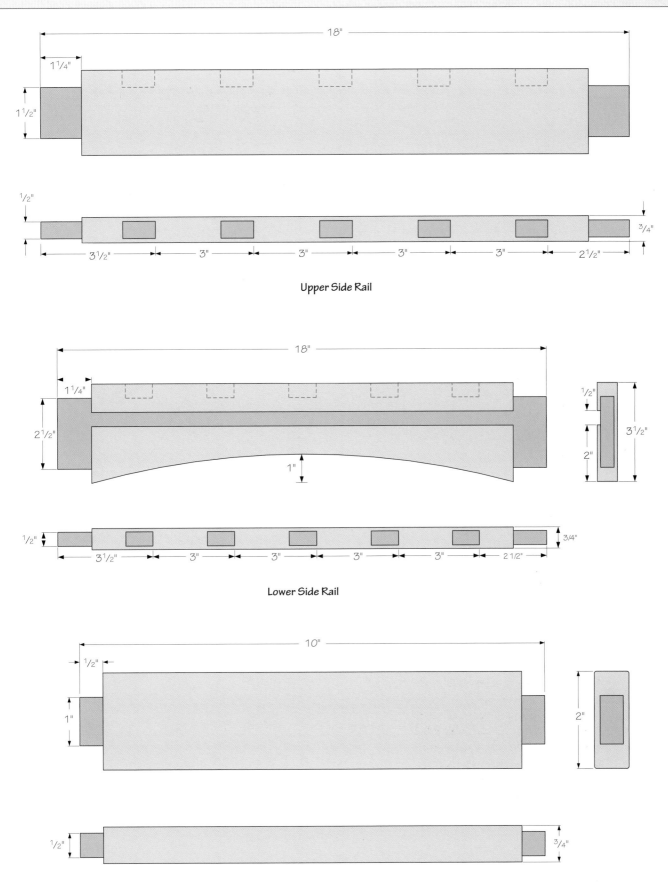

Upper Side Rail

Lower Side Rail

Side Stile

3 Lay out and cut the mortises in the side rails. Then, using a tenoning fixture, set the thickness of the tenons by making cheek cuts. Fit the tenons on the side stiles to the mortises in the side rails. Fit the tenons on the side rails to the mortises in the ends.

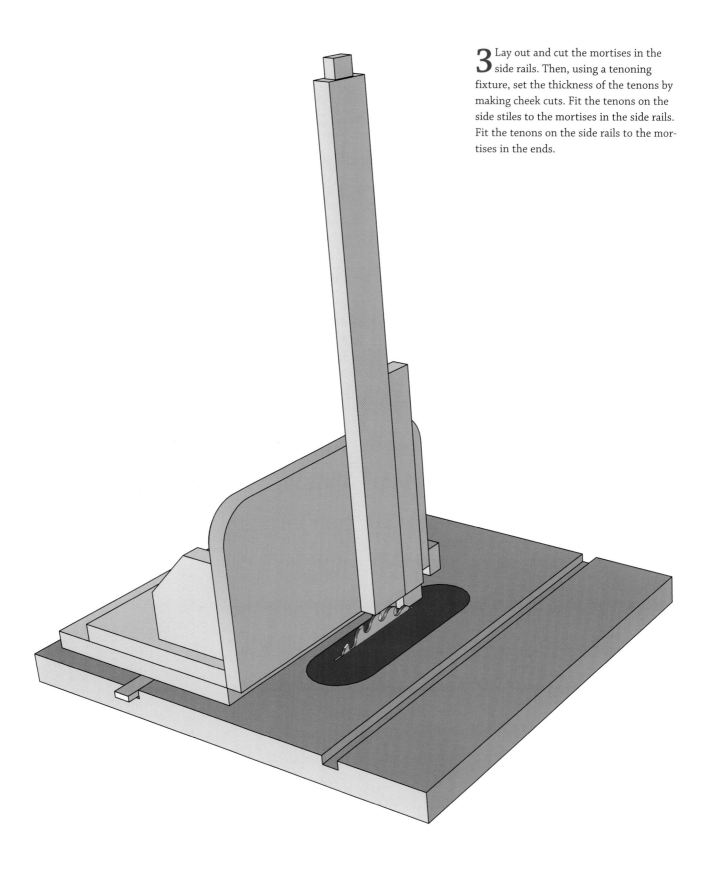

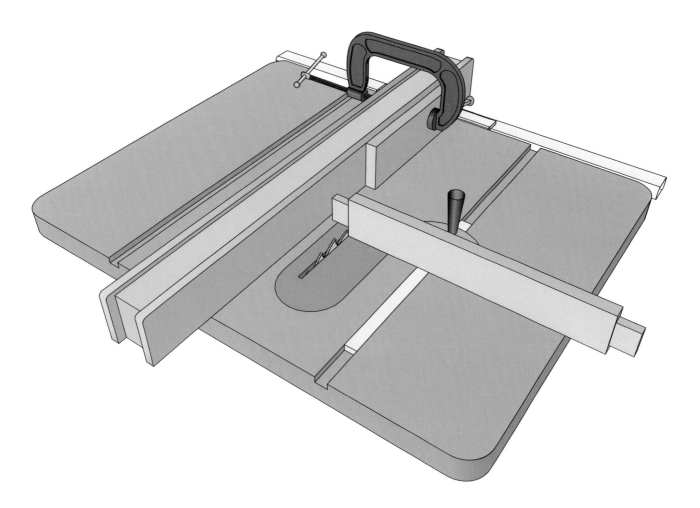

4 Use a stop block clamped to your table saw fence to set the length of the tenons. Make the shoulder cuts, then nibble away the material to form the tenon.

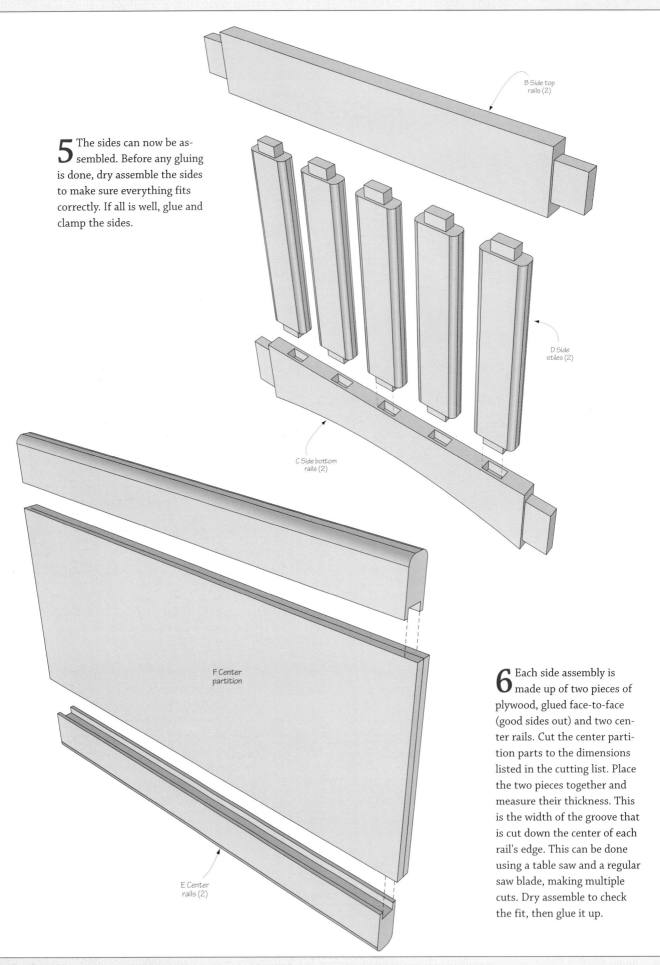

5 The sides can now be assembled. Before any gluing is done, dry assemble the sides to make sure everything fits correctly. If all is well, glue and clamp the sides.

B Side top rails (2)

D Side stiles (2)

C Side bottom rails (2)

F Center partition

6 Each side assembly is made up of two pieces of plywood, glued face-to-face (good sides out) and two center rails. Cut the center partition parts to the dimensions listed in the cutting list. Place the two pieces together and measure their thickness. This is the width of the groove that is cut down the center of each rail's edge. This can be done using a table saw and a regular saw blade, making multiple cuts. Dry assemble to check the fit, then glue it up.

E Center rails (2)

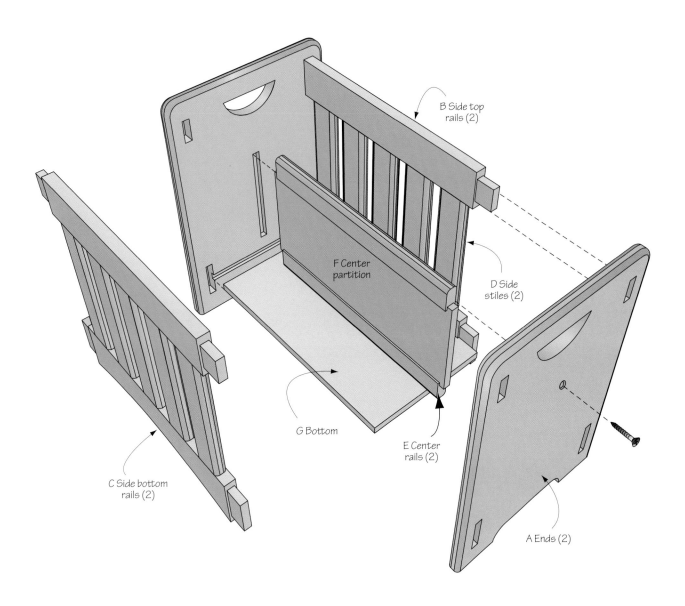

B Side top
rails (2)

F Center
partition

D Side
stiles (2)

G Bottom

E Center
rails (2)

C Side bottom
rails (2)

A Ends (2)

7 Dry assemble the rack and measure the distance between the dadoes in each end. This is the exact length of the bottom. Fine tune the fit of the bottom if necessary. Assemble the rack. Insert a screw through the end and into the end of the top rail. Flip the rack over and install two screws through the bottom and into the bottom rail.

OCTAGONAL TAVERN TABLE

Most likely the origins of an octagonal table like this project can be traced to an old pub with a British gentleman sitting there, drinking a pint and resting the tankard on the little octagon table beside him.

Today, placed beside a sofa or an easy chair, this table is an ideal place for a lamp. And, it has a shelf to hold books or magazines. This project is made of cherry, but oak would also be a good wood to use.

inches (millimeters)

REFERENCE	QUANTITY	PART	STOCK	THICKNESS	(mm)	WIDTH	(mm)	LENGTH	(mm)	COMMENTS
A	1	top	hardwood	¾	(19)	17	(432)	17	(432)	
B	4	posts	hardwood	¾	(19)	2¾	(70)	24¾	(629)	
C	4	feet	hardwood	1½	(38)	1½	(38)	7	(178)	
D	2	upper crosspieces	hardwood	¾	(19)	1½	(38)	12	(305)	
E	2	lower crosspieces	hardwood	¾	(19)	1½	(38)	12	(305)	
F	1	shelf	hardwood	¾	(19)	11³⁄₁₆	(284)	11³⁄₁₆	(284)	cut to fit between posts

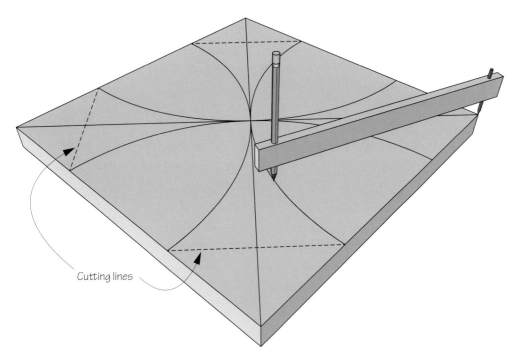

Cutting lines

1 Square up the blank for the top. Draw two diagonals from corner to corner. This will determine the center of the blank. Use your compass or trammel points and scribe a semi circle from each corner to the center. Connect the points where the semi circles cross the edges of the blank. You now have the outline of an octagon. Set the miter gauge of your table saw to 45 degrees and cut off four corners. Round over the top and bottom edges using a ¼"-roundover router bit.

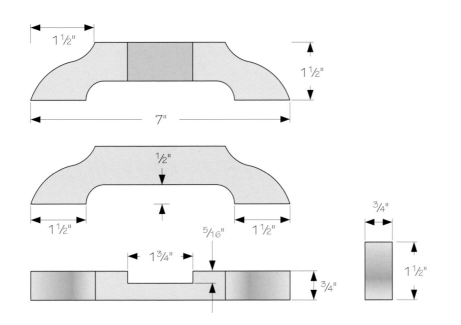

2 Each foot is made from two pieces of wood. The illustration shows one half of a foot. Cut four blanks oversize and glue two halves together to form the two foot blanks. Square these blanks and cut them to size. Cut the dadoes using a dado blade in your table saw. Or, you could set up a straight-cutting bit in a router table and cut the dadoes. Lay out and cut the curves using a band saw or jigsaw.

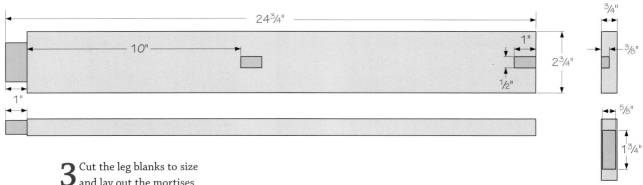

3 Cut the leg blanks to size and lay out the mortises and tenon. Cut the mortises with a mortiser or drill holes using a ½"-Forstner bit and clean them up with a chisel. Cut the notches with a chisel. Using a ¼"-roundover router bit, rout the long edges of the legs. Cut the tenons to fit the through mortises in the feet.

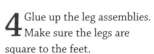

4 Glue up the leg assemblies. Make sure the legs are square to the feet.

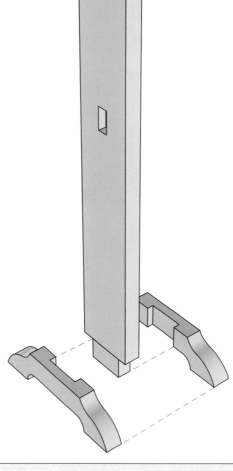

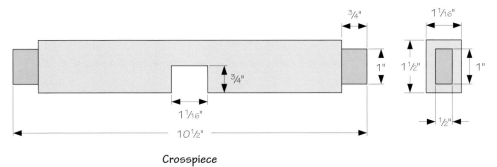

Crosspiece

5 Cut the upper and lower crosspiece blanks to size. Cut and fit the tenons for the leg mortises. Cut the notches in the middle of each crosspiece to create a lap joint. Screw the crosspieces together.

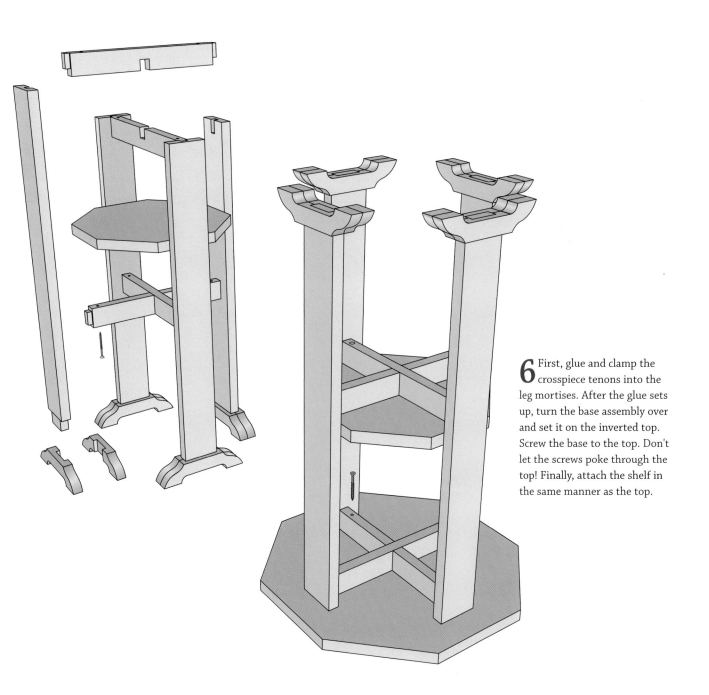

6 First, glue and clamp the crosspiece tenons into the leg mortises. After the glue sets up, turn the base assembly over and set it on the inverted top. Screw the base to the top. Don't let the screws poke through the top! Finally, attach the shelf in the same manner as the top.

TRESTLE BENCH

One of the characteristics of Arts & Crafts furniture has always been "simplicity of form", as well as "quality of craftsmanship". This bench exhibits these principles, and, slightly departs from the original Mission feature of looking somewhat square in shape. The side assemblies have a curved shape at the bottom of each, and all edges of the bench are rounded over. These two things tend to soften the design, and make it more pleasing to the eyes.

This bench will fit fine in a foyer, hallway or a pair of these could serve as benches for a dining table. Made from 5/4 cherry, and given a Danish oil finish, it should give many years of service.

inches (millimeters)

REFERENCE	QUANTITY	PART	STOCK	THICKNESS	(mm)	WIDTH	(mm)	LENGTH	(mm)	COMMENTS
A	1	seat	hardwood	1¹⁄₁₆	(27)	12	(305)	60	(1524)	
B	1	cross bar	hardwood	1¹⁄₁₆	(27)	3	(76)	58	(147)	
C	2	ends	hardwood	1¹⁄₁₆	(27)	11	(279)	16	(406)	
D	2	top cleats	hardwood	2¹⁄₈	(54)	2	(51)	10	(254)	
E	2	wedges	hardwood	¼	(6)	1¹⁄₈	(29)	4	(102)	
F	4	seat side supports	hardwood	1¹⁄₁₆	(27)	2	(51)	10	(254)	

1 After laying out the mortises, tenons and decorative curve, use a ¾"-Forstner bit and rough out the through mortises. These can then be squared up with a mallet and chisel. Cut the shoulders for the tenons at the top of each end piece. Use your table saw to cut the shoulders about ⅛" deep. Remove the bulk of the wood, by using a stacked dado head installed in the table saw, or simply nibble away the material to form the tenon. Lay out the 6" tenon and cut off the waste with the band saw.

Cut the radius and taper the side using the band saw. Smooth the tapered sides using a jointer or hand plane. Round over the side and curved edges with a ¼"-roundover router bit.

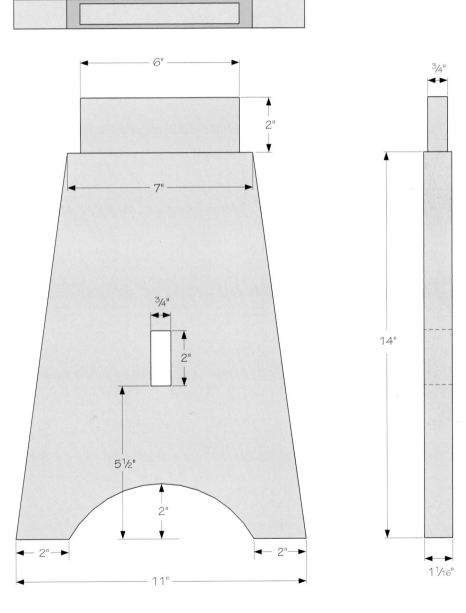

End

2 Each cleat is made of two pieces. They will be put together at final assembly. Cut the dadoes on your table saw and cut the curve ends on a band saw.

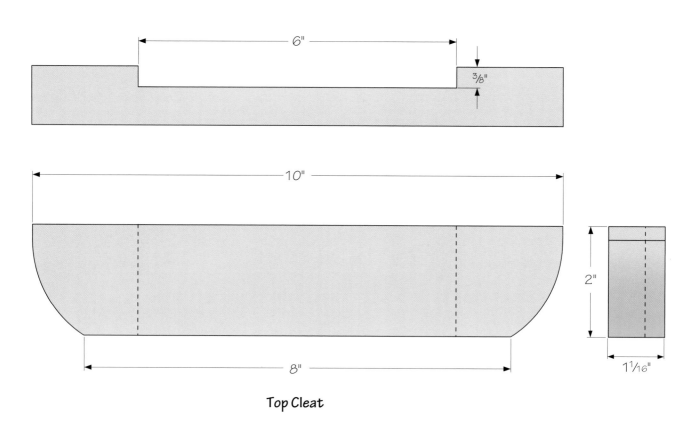

Top Cleat

3 Cut the tenons on a table saw and round the ends of the tenons using a band saw. Cut a tapered mortise in each mortise using a ¼"-Forstner bit and a hammer and chisel. These mortises will house the wedges.

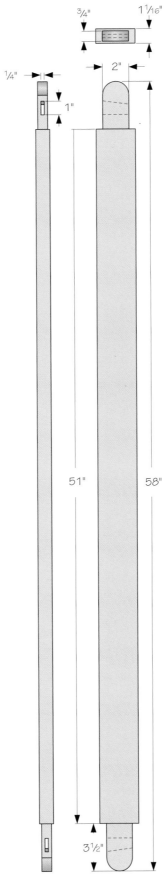

Cross Bar

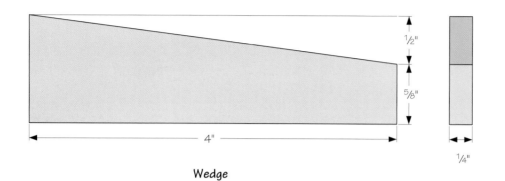

½"

⅝"

4"

¼"

Wedge

4 Cut the wedges to shape. These will be fitted to the mortises in the crossbar during final assembly.

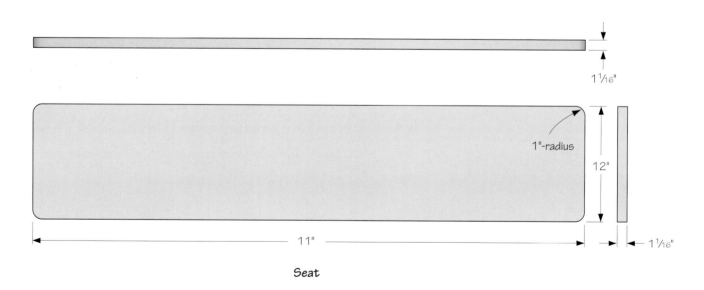

1 ¹⁄₁₆"

1"-radius

12"

11"

1 ¹⁄₁₆"

Seat

5 If necessary, glue up boards to create a 12"-wide board. Cut the seat to size and cut the radii on the corners using a jig saw.

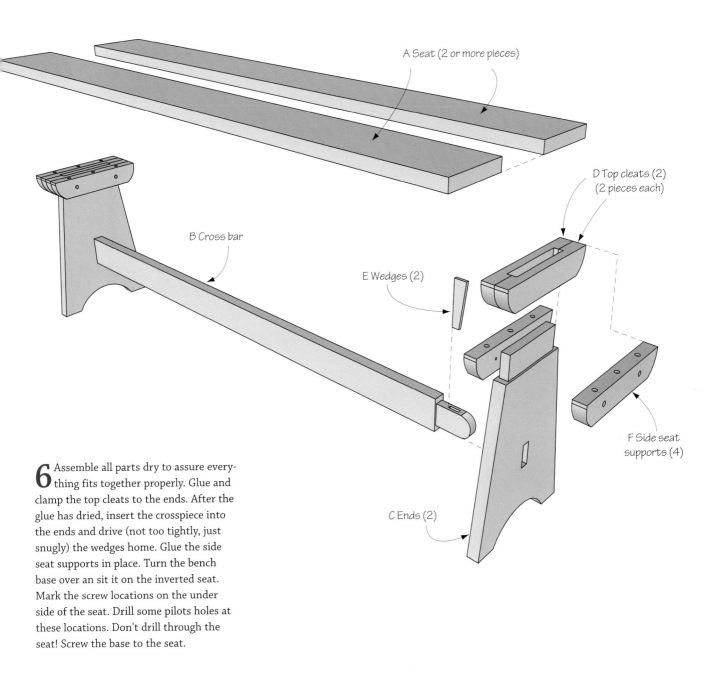

A Seat (2 or more pieces)

D Top cleats (2)
(2 pieces each)

B Cross bar

E Wedges (2)

F Side seat
supports (4)

C Ends (2)

6 Assemble all parts dry to assure everything fits together properly. Glue and clamp the top cleats to the ends. After the glue has dried, insert the crosspiece into the ends and drive (not too tightly, just snugly) the wedges home. Glue the side seat supports in place. Turn the bench base over an sit it on the inverted seat. Mark the screw locations on the under side of the seat. Drill some pilots holes at these locations. Don't drill through the seat! Screw the base to the seat.

OCTAGONAL TABOURET TABLE

This delightful little table will fit into any setting. It is similar to the Octagonal Tavern Table, with the exceptions that it is not as tall, doesn't have a shelf and it has straight legs with no feet. It's made of cherry wood and features mortise-and-tenon joinery. This is a fun project to build.

inches (millimeters)

REFERENCE	QUANTITY	PART	STOCK	THICKNESS	(mm)	WIDTH	(mm)	LENGTH	(mm)	COMMENTS
A	1	top	hardwood	1¹/₁₆	(27)	15	(381)	15	(381)	
B	4	legs	hardwood	1³/₄	(44)	1³/₄	(44)	16	(406)	
C	4	crosspieces	hardwood	1¹/₁₆	(27)	2¹/₂	(64)	10¹/₂	(267)	
D	8	dowels	hardwood	³/₈ d	(9.5)	1	(25)			

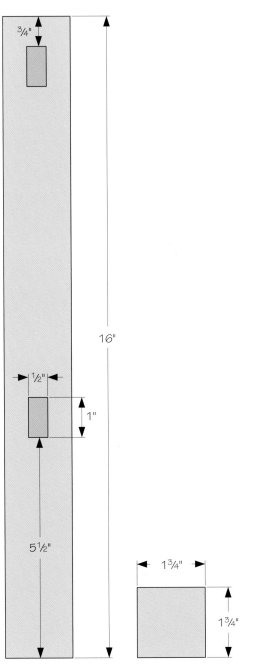

1 The legs can made from 8/4 stock, or if you don't have any, you can glue up enough 4/4 to make the leg blanks. After laying out and cutting the mortises, use a ³/₈"-roundover router bit on all the long edges of each leg.

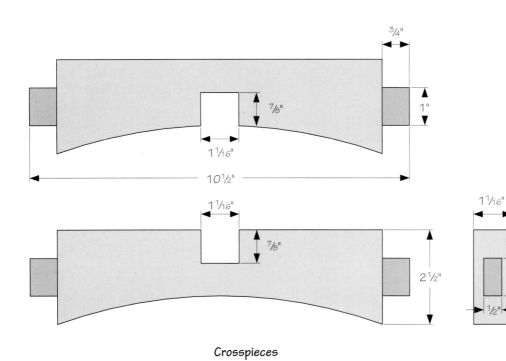

3/4"

7/8"

1"

1 1/16"

10 1/2"

1 1/16"

7/8"

2 1/2"

1 1/16"

1"

1/2"

Crosspieces

2 Cut the crosspiece blanks to size. Cut the tenons to fit the leg mortises. Cut the notches using a dado blade in your table saw. Cut one dado 7/8" deep and the other dado 1 7/8" deep. Lay out the curves. Make two crosspieces each as shown in the illustration.

3 Cut to top blank to size and lay out the octagon. The method shown in the illustration is a clever way of dividing a square into eight equal faces.

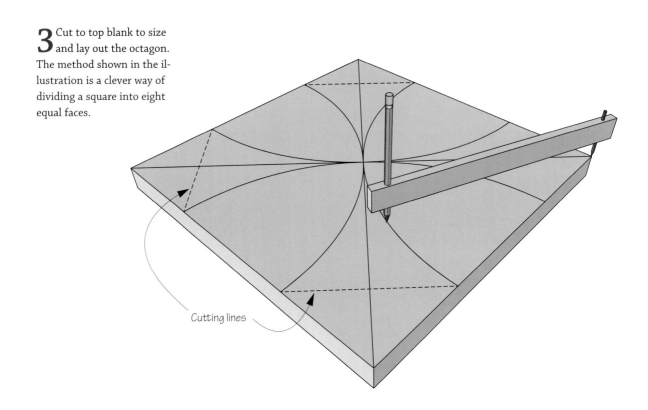

Cutting lines

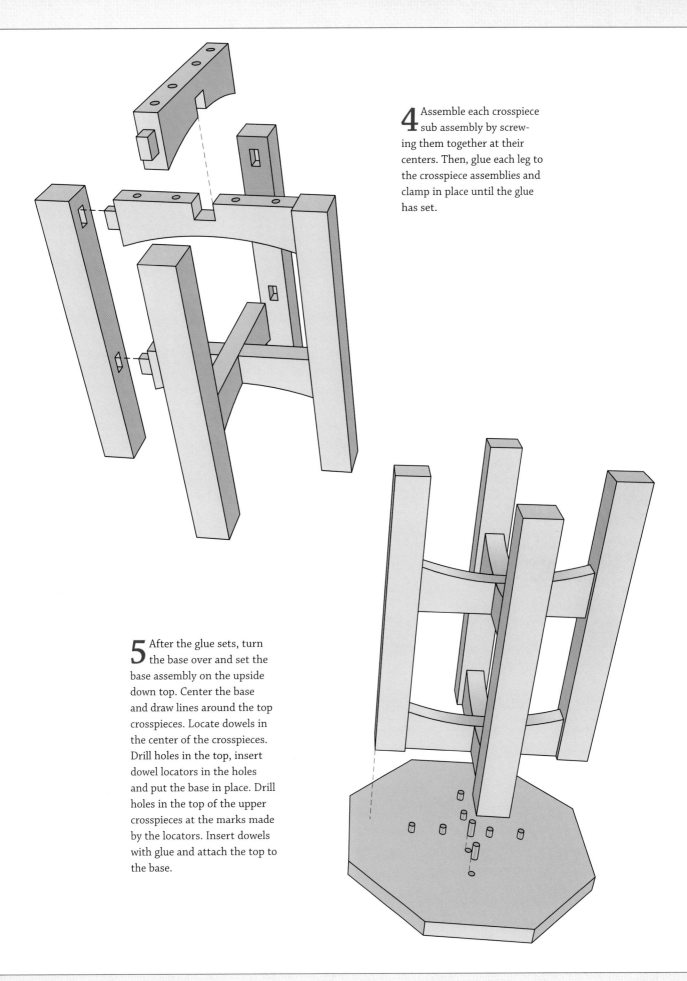

4 Assemble each crosspiece sub assembly by screwing them together at their centers. Then, glue each leg to the crosspiece assemblies and clamp in place until the glue has set.

5 After the glue sets, turn the base over and set the base assembly on the upside down top. Center the base and draw lines around the top crosspieces. Locate dowels in the center of the crosspieces. Drill holes in the top, insert dowel locators in the holes and put the base in place. Drill holes in the top of the upper crosspieces at the marks made by the locators. Insert dowels with glue and attach the top to the base.

MISSION-STYLE DESKTOP BOOK RACK

Placed on a desk, this book rack has enough room to hold all the books you'll need to do that particular research project. Made from cherry, and finished with Danish oil, this is a relatively easy project to build.

inches (millimeters)

REFERENCE	QUANTITY	PART	STOCK	THICKNESS	(mm)	WIDTH	(mm)	LENGTH	(mm)	COMMENTS
A	2	sides	hardwood	¾	(19)	7	(178)	7	(178)	
B	1	platform	hardwood	¾	(19)	6¾	(171)	25	(635)	
C	1	1	hardwood	¾	(19)	¾	(19)	21	(533)	
D	4	wedges	hardwood	¼	(6)	¾	(19)	2½	(63.5)	

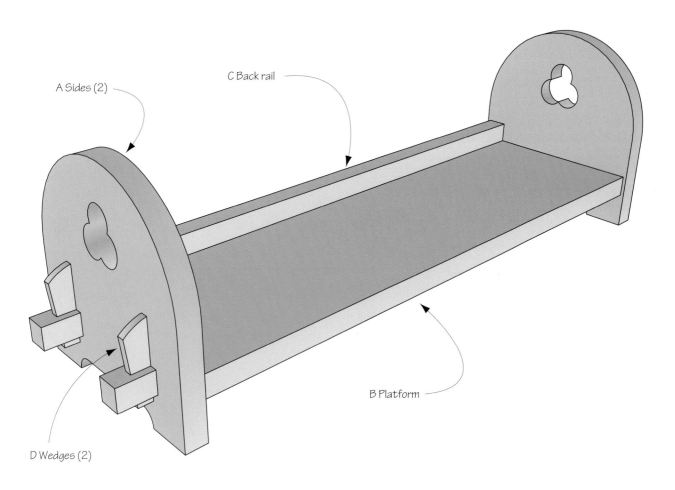

A Sides (2)

C Back rail

B Platform

D Wedges (2)

1 On the side blanks, lay out the decorative cutout, through mortises and the cutout that creates the feet.

Next, lay out all the tenons and tapered mortises on the platform.

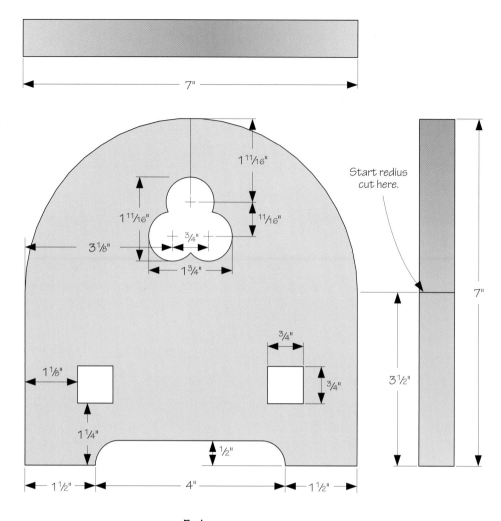

7"

1 11/16"

11/16"

1 11/16"

3 1/8"

3/4"

1 3/4"

3/4"

3/4"

1 1/8"

3/4"

1 1/4"

1/2"

1 1/2" 4" 1 1/2"

Start redius cut here.

7"

3 1/2"

End

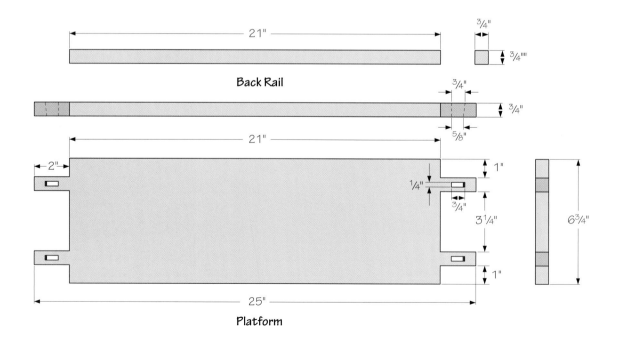

21"

3/4"

3/4""

Back Rail

3/4"

3/4"

21"

5/8"

2"

1"

1/4"

3/4"

3/4"

3 1/4"

6 3/4"

1"

25"

Platform

2 Use a 1" Forstner bit to create the clo-ver-leaf design. Use a ¾"-Forstner bit to drill the through mortises, then square them up with a chisel.

3 Cut the tenons on the platform using a table saw or band saw. Fit them to the mortises in the sides. Cut the tapered mortises by first drilling the through mortise, then use a chisel to square up and create the taper in the mortise.

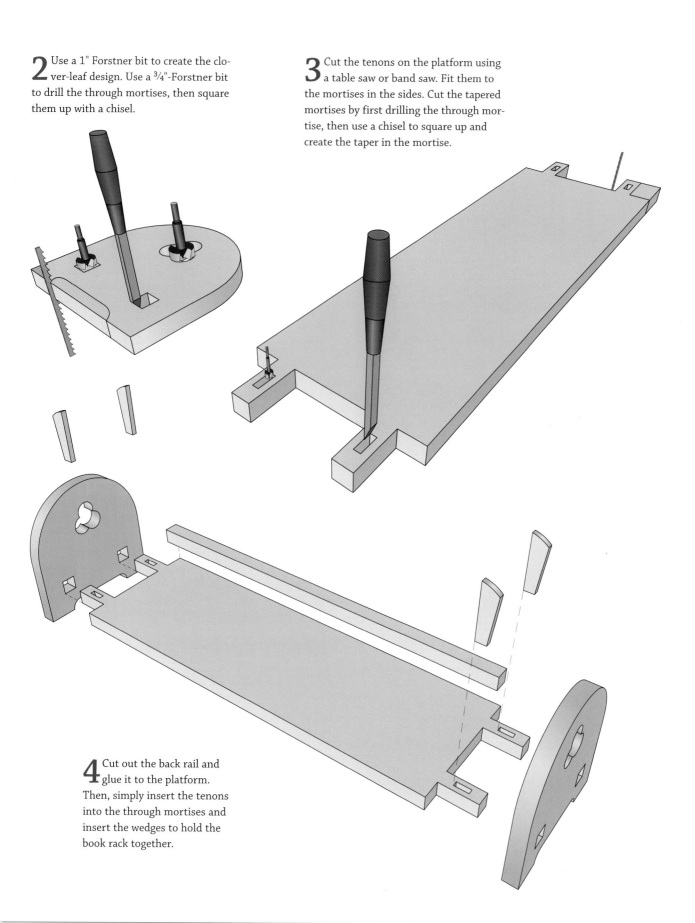

4 Cut out the back rail and glue it to the platform. Then, simply insert the tenons into the through mortises and insert the wedges to hold the book rack together.

MISSION-STYLE REVOLVING BOOKCASE

I have never seen a revolving bookcase in any of the early Mission, or Arts & Crafts catalogs, (I don't think they had the means of making it revolve easily). This bookcase is designed and built in the Arts & Crafts tradition. Placed next to a desk or in the living room, it will hold many books and compliment any setting. The revolving bookcase puts the books at your fingertips.

Oak is a good wood to use for this project. It can be stained to a soft golden oak and finished with an acrylic varnish. Cherry can also be used and left in its natural shade or given a slight tint.

It's possible and easier to finish this project before final assembly. Mask off the areas that will have glue applied to them (for example, the mortises and tenons). Finish all the parts, then assemble the bookcase.

inches (millimeters)

REFERENCE	QUANTITY	PART	STOCK	THICKNESS	(mm)	WIDTH	(mm)	LENGTH	(mm)	COMMENTS
A	1	top	plywood	³⁄₄	(19)	21³⁄₄	(553)	21³⁄₄	(553)	
B	4	top border	hardwood	³⁄₄	(19)	³⁄₄	(19)	22³⁄₄	(578)	
C	1	middle shelf	plywood	³⁄₄	(19)	19³⁄₄	(502)	19³⁄₄	(502)	
D	4	middle shelf border	hardwood	³⁄₄	(19)	³⁄₄	(19)	20³⁄₄	(527)	
E	1	sub top	plywood	³⁄₄	(19)	21	(533)	21	(533)	
E	1	bottom shelf	plywood	³⁄₄	(19)	21	(533)	21	(533)	
F	4	middle shelf border	hardwood	³⁄₄	(19)	³⁄₄	(19)	20³⁄₄	(527)	
G	8	upper/lower aprons	hardwood	³⁄₄	(19)	1¹⁄₂	(38)	22	(559)	
H	2	upper post assembly	hardwood	³⁄₄	(19)	4	(102)	11¹⁄₄	(286)	
I	2	lower post assembly	hardwood	³⁄₄	(19)	4	(102)	12	(305)	
J	20	stringer	hardwood	¹⁄₂	(13)	1	(25)	23¹⁄₂	(597)	
K	4	lower divider	hardwood	³⁄₄	(19)	1¹⁄₂	(38)	8³⁄₈	(213)	
L	4	upper divider	hardwood	³⁄₄	(19)	1¹⁄₂	(38)	7³⁄₄	(197)	
M	1	floor platform	hardwood	³⁄₄	(19)	18	(457)	18	(457)	
N	1	bearing plate	plywood	¹⁄₂	(13)	9	(229)	9	(229)	
O	1	6" Lazy Susan bearing								Woodcraft #02Z41 or equivalent

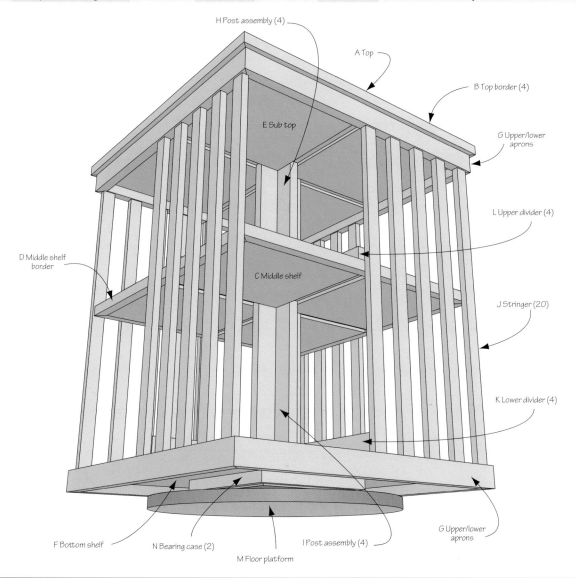

1 Cut out all the border strips and aprons. Then cut the groove down the length of each top border using a table saw with a dado blade or a router (mounted under a table) with a straight bit. See the illustrations for locations of the grooves. Cut the grooves in the top with a router, a straight-cutting bit and a straightedge to guide the router.

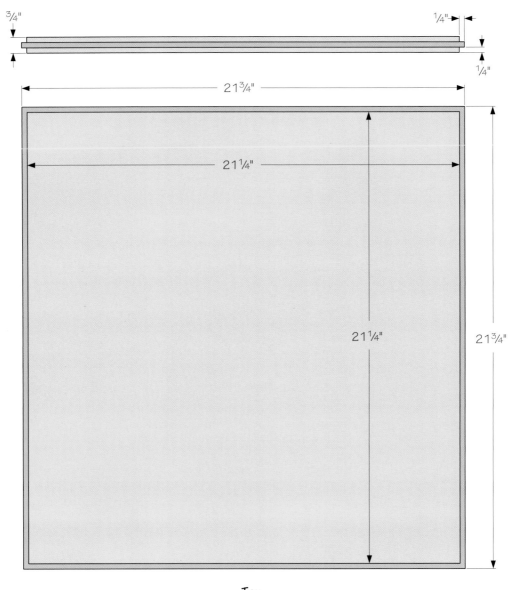

3/4"   1/4"   1/4"

21³⁄₄"

21¹⁄₄"

21¹⁄₄"

21³⁄₄"

Top

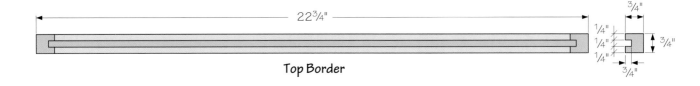

22³⁄₄"

3/4"

1/4"
1/4"
1/4"

3/4"

3/4"

Top Border

2 Now, cut the top, subtop, middle shelf and bottom shelf blanks to size. Cut the rabbets around the edges of each blank using a table saw with a dado head or using a router and a rabbet-cutting bit. The lip on each piece needs to fit into its corresponding groove in the apron parts. Cut the grooves in the parts using a router, a straight-cutting bit and a straightedge to guide the router. Cut the mortises in the top and bottom aprons. Remember that the top and bottom aprons are mirror images of each other.

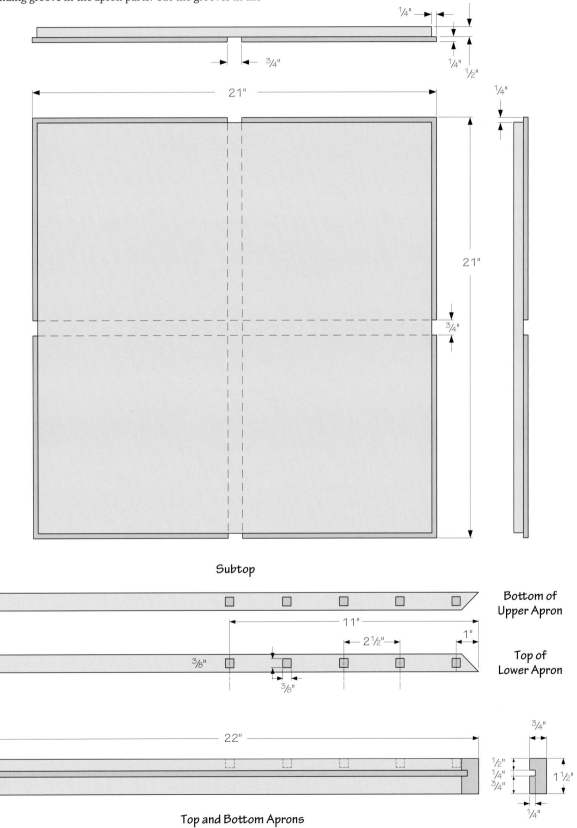

Subtop

Bottom of
Upper Apron

Top of
Lower Apron

Top and Bottom Aprons

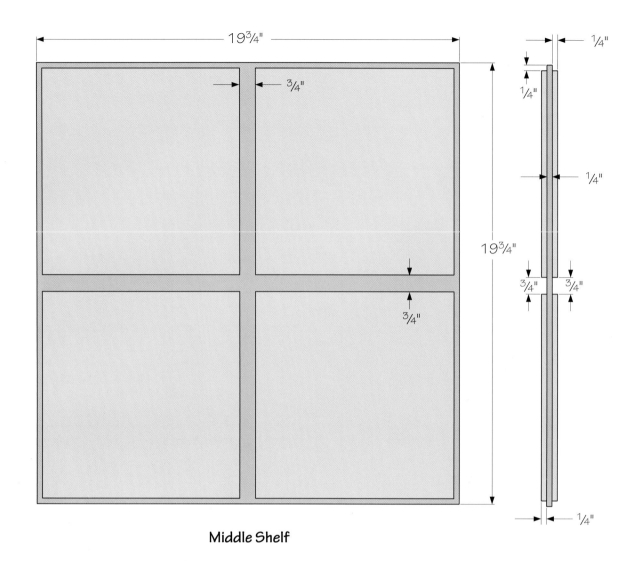

Middle Shelf

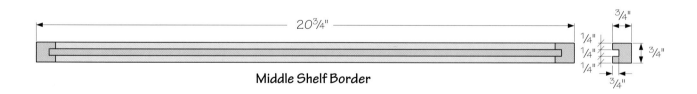

Middle Shelf Border

3 Cut a 45-degree miter on the end of each edging and apron part and fit them to each corresponding shelf, top and subtop. Attach the edgings and aprons in place using glue and clamps.

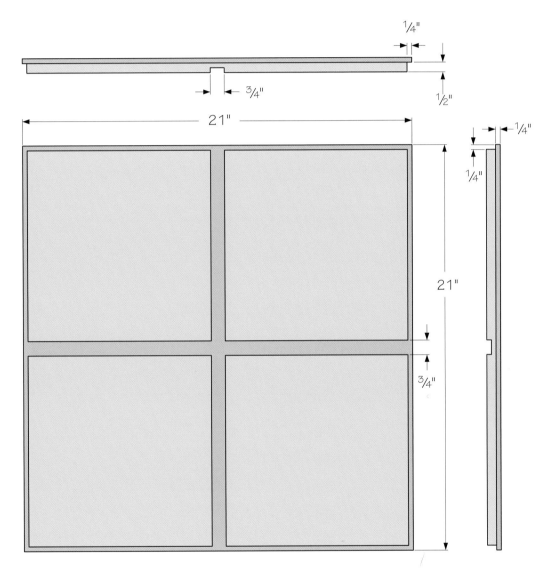

Bottom Shelf

4 Cut out the lower and upper dividers and the posts. Cut the notches in the posts using a band saw or jigsaw. Then cut out the stringer blanks and cut the tenons on each end of the stringers using a table saw. These tenons need to fit the mortises in the upper and lower aprons.

7⅝"

1½"

¾"

Upper Divider

8¼"

1½"

¾"

Lower Divider

4"

¾"

¾"

6"

12"

Post

3/8"   3/8"

¼"

22½"

1"   ½"

Stringer

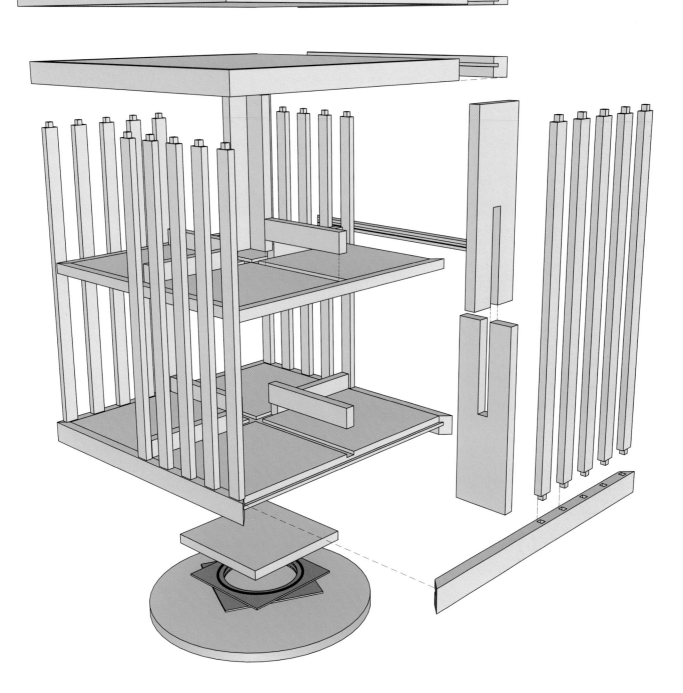

5 Fit the lower post assembly to the bottom shelf. Drill four pilot holes from the underneath side of the bottom shelf. Now glue and screw the upper post assembly to the subtop in the same manner.

First, set the bottom assembly on your worktop. Then, glue and insert the stringers in the bottom mortises. Add glue to the tops of the lower posts and the lower stringers and place the middle shelf on the bottom assembly, installing the tenons in the mortises in the bottom edge of the middle shelf apron. Make sure the grain is running the same direction on each shelf.

Add glue to the top tenons on the stringers and tops of the upper posts. Put the subtop assembly on the middle shelf assembly and line up the tenons of the stringers with the mortises in the middle shelf apron.

To add additional strength to the bookcase, apply a little glue and nail a small brad through each stringer where it meets the edge of the middle shelf. Now glue the dividers in place.

Screw the bearing plate to the bottom of the bookcase. Follow the mounting instructions for mounting the bearing assembly to the floor platform and the bearing plate.

SOFA SIDE TABLE

This side table will fit perfectly next to your sofa or easy chair, allowing you to have your most-used items within reach. The shelf makes an excellent place for books or magazines.

Cherry is a good choice of wood for this project. It can be left in its natural shade or given a slight tint.

It's easier to finish this project before final assembly. Mask off the areas that will have glue applied to them (for example, the mortises and tenons). Finish all the parts, then assemble the side table.

inches (millimeters)

REFERENCE	QUANTITY	PART	STOCK	THICKNESS	(mm)	WIDTH	(mm)	LENGTH	(mm)	COMMENTS
A	1	top	hardwood	¾	(19)	13½	(343)	26	(660)	
B	2	top cleats	hardwood	1¹⁄₁₆	(27)	2	(51)	10	(254)	
C	2	feet	hardwood	1¹⁄₁₆	(27)	3	(76)	13½	(343)	
D	4	side uprights	hardwood	¾	(19)	2	(51)	22¾	(578)	
E	2	shelves	hardwood	¾	(19)	6¼	(159)	24	(610)	
F	8	wedges	hardwood	⅜	(10)	2	(51)	2	(51)	
	4	dowels	hardwood	⅜ d	(10)	¾	(19)			

A Top

B Top cleat (2)

E Shelf (2)

D Side upright (4)

F Wedge (8)

C Foot (2)

1 Cut and joint the wood to make up the top to the dimensions listed in the bill of materials. Glue and clamp these boards. When the glue has dried, size the board to final dimension. Sand the board and round over the top edges with a ¼"-roundover bit.

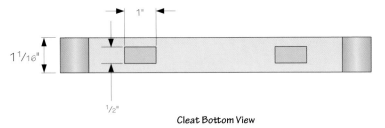

Cleat Profile View

2 The cleats are made from 5/4 material. Cut the blanks to dimension. On the bottom edge, lay out and cut the mortises. Cut a 1" radius on the bottom corners. As shown in the drawing, bore two, ⅜"-diameter holes in the top, ⅜" deep.

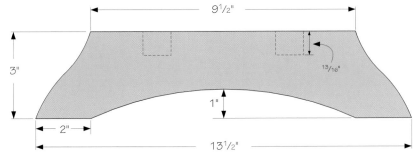

Cleat Bottom View

3 The feet are also made from 5/4 material. Cut the blanks to dimension. On the top edge, lay out and cut the mortises. Lay out and cut the curves on the ends and bottom with a band saw.

Foot Profile View

Foot Top View

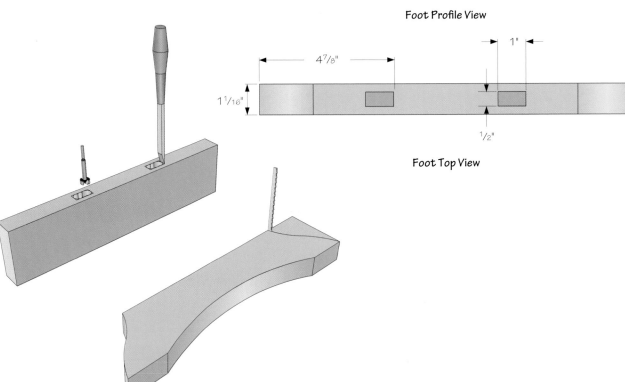

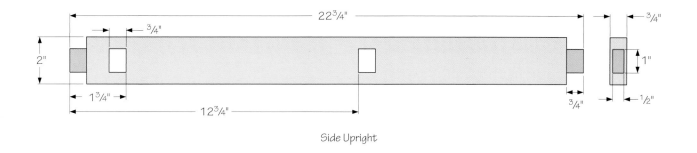

Side Upright

4 Cut the uprights to finished dimensions. Lay out the tenons on each end as shown in the drawing. To cut the tenons, use a tenoning fixture on your table saw. Double check the fit of these tenons in the mortises in the feet and upper cleats. Now lay out the mortises and cut them using a 1"-Forstner bit, then trim them square using a chisel.

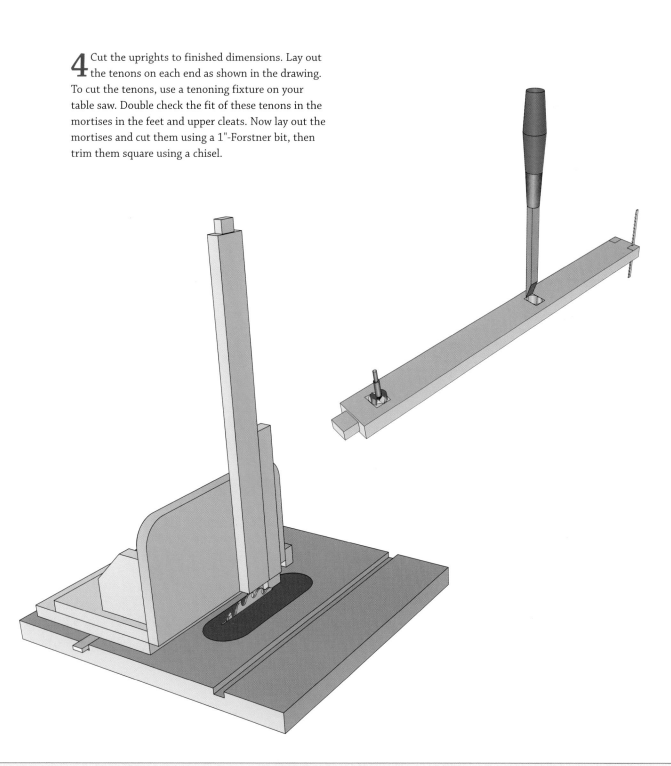

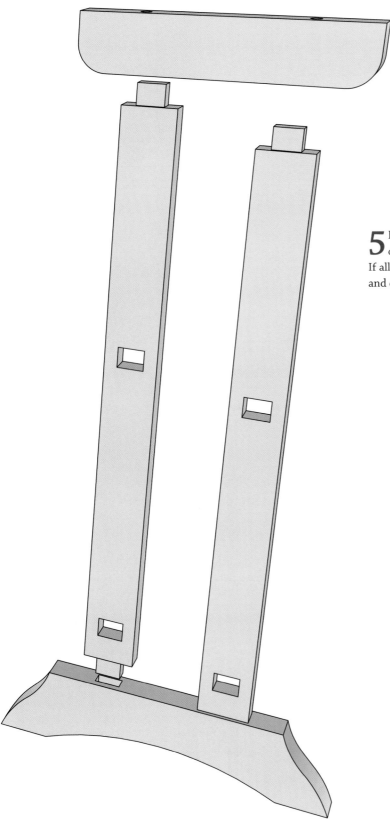

5 Dry assemble the two uprights to a cleat and a foot and check for proper fit. If all is well, these parts can now be glued and clamped. Make two of these assemblies.

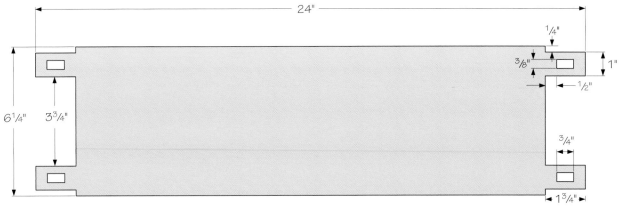

Shelf

6 Cut the two shelves to final dimensions and lay out the tenons on either end of the shelves. These tenons will fit into the through mortises in the uprights. The tenons can be cut on a band saw. Each tenon has a ³⁄₈"-through mortise.

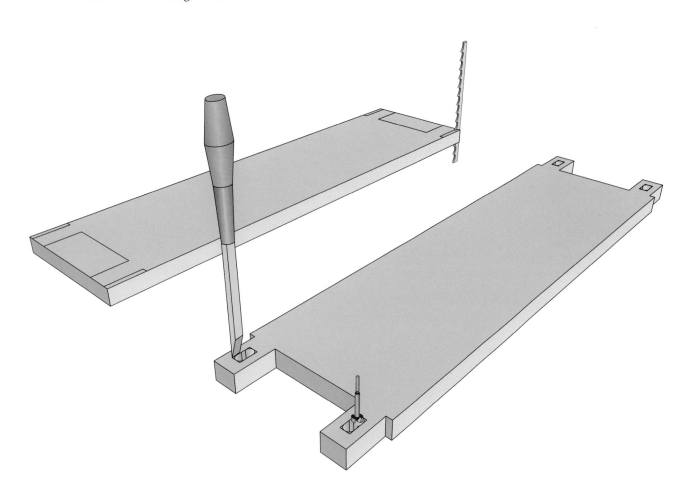

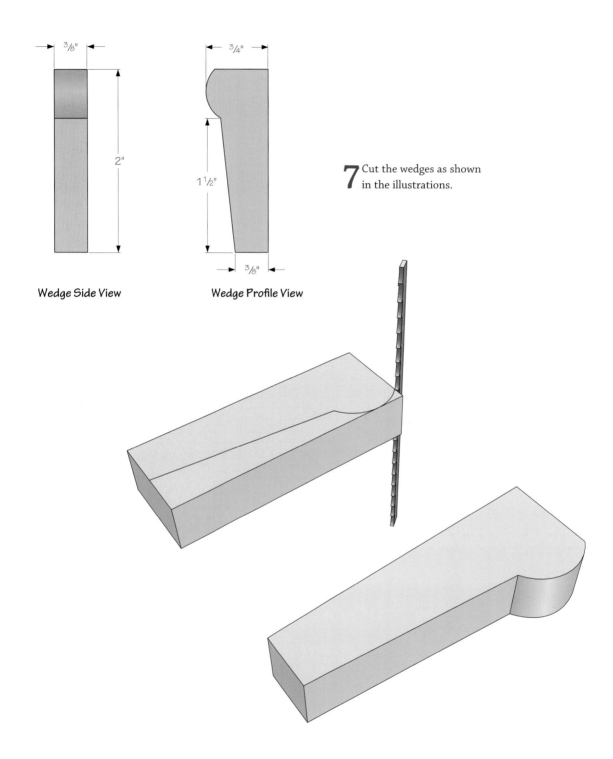

$^3/_8$"

2"

Wedge Side View

$^3/_4$"

$1^1/_2$"

$^3/_8$"

Wedge Profile View

7 Cut the wedges as shown in the illustrations.

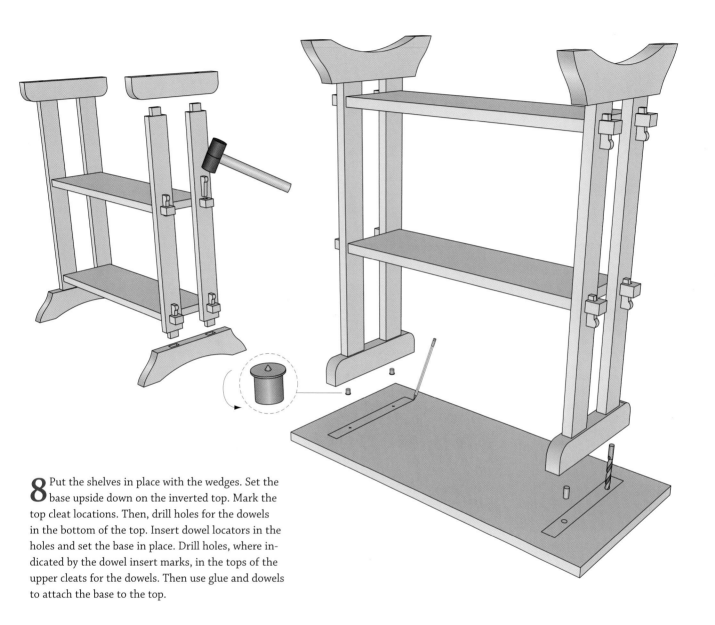

8 Put the shelves in place with the wedges. Set the base upside down on the inverted top. Mark the top cleat locations. Then, drill holes for the dowels in the bottom of the top. Insert dowel locators in the holes and set the base in place. Drill holes, where indicated by the dowel insert marks, in the tops of the upper cleats for the dowels. Then use glue and dowels to attach the base to the top.

ÉTAGÈRE WITH ADJUSTABLE SHELVES

An   is defined as a stand with open shelves that is used to display small objets d'art or ornaments. This project is designed in the Arts & Crafts tradition, with small curved aprons and lots of vertical stringers. The curved aprons tend to break up the otherwise square look of the étagère.

Principal uses for this étagère were to hold items such as clean towels, wash cloths and other sundry items found in the bathroom, but it would look great in any room in the house.

This project is made of cherry wood and given a natural-color finish using several coats of tung oil.

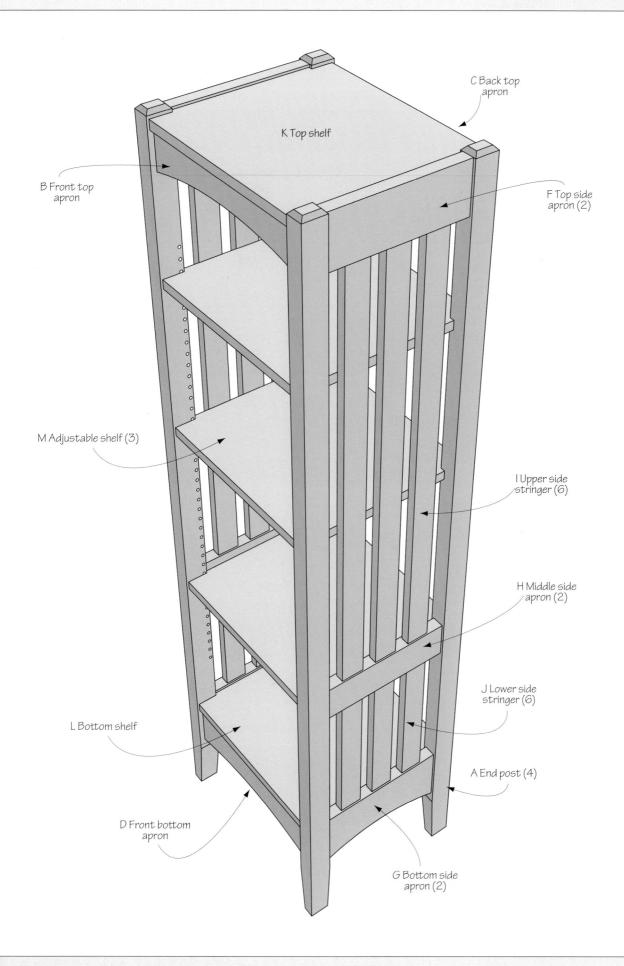

C Back top apron

K Top shelf

B Front top apron

F Top side apron (2)

M Adjustable shelf (3)

I Upper side stringer (6)

H Middle side apron (2)

J Lower side stringer (6)

L Bottom shelf

A End post (4)

D Front bottom apron

G Bottom side apron (2)

inches (millimeters)

REFERENCE	QUANTITY	PART	STOCK	THICKNESS	(mm)	WIDTH	(mm)	LENGTH	(mm)	COMMENTS
A	4	legs	hardwood	1³/₄	(44)	2	(51)	66	(168)	make 2 right and 2 left end posts
B	1	front top apron	hardwood	1¹/₁₆	(27)	3	(76)	17¹/₂	(446)	
C	1	back top apron	hardwood	1¹/₁₆	(27)	3	(76)	17¹/₂	(446)	
D	4	front bottom apron	hardwood	1¹/₁₆	(27)	4	(102)	17¹/₂	(446)	
E	1	back bottom apron	hardwood	1¹/₁₆	(27)	4	(102)	17¹/₂	(446)	
F	2	top side aprons	hardwood	1¹/₁₆	(27)	4	(102)	13	(330)	
G	2	bottom side aprons	hardwood	1¹/₁₆	(27)	5	(127)	13	(330)	
H	2	middle side aprons	hardwood	1¹/₁₆	(27)	3	(76)	13	(330)	
I	6	upper side stringers	hardwood	³/₄	(19)	2	(51)	36¹/₂	(927)	
J	6	lower side stringers	hardwood	³/₄	(19)	2	(51)	14	(356)	
K	1	top shelf	hardwood	³/₄	(19)	15	(381)	17¹³/₁₆	(452)	cut to fit
L	1	bottom shelf	hardwood	³/₄	(19)	15	(381)	17¹³/₁₆	(452)	cut to fit
M	3	adjustable shelves	hardwood	³/₄	(19)	15	(381)	17¹³/₁₆	(452)	cut to fit
	16	tabletop fasteners								Woodcraft #27N10 or equivalent
	12	shelf supports								Woodcraft #27114 or equivalent

1 Cut out the front and back, top and bottom aprons. Wait to cut the tenons until you've cut the mortises in the legs. Then, fit the tenons to the mortises in the legs. Finally, cut the curves using a band saw or jigsaw. Sand the curves smooth.

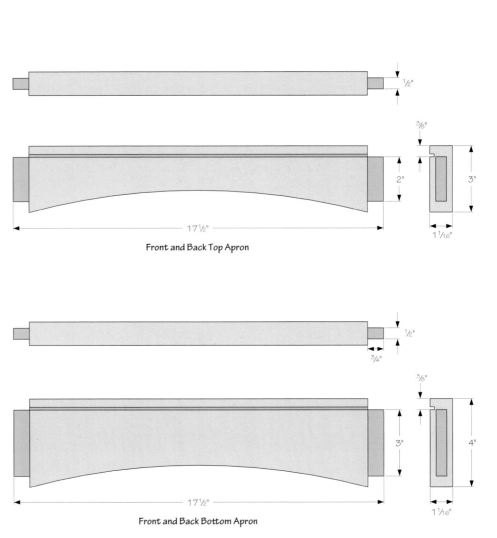

Front and Back Top Apron

Front and Back Bottom Apron

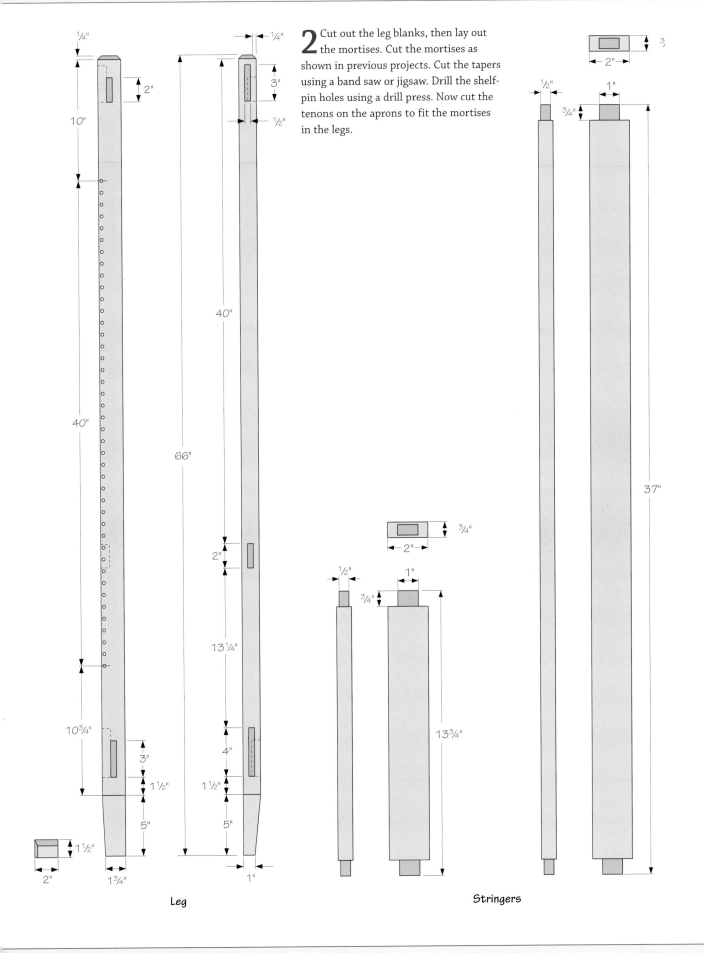

2 Cut out the leg blanks, then lay out the mortises. Cut the mortises as shown in previous projects. Cut the tapers using a band saw or jigsaw. Drill the shelf-pin holes using a drill press. Now cut the tenons on the aprons to fit the mortises in the legs.

Leg

Stringers

3 Cut out the top, middle and bottom side aprons. Cut the tenons to fit the mortises in the legs. Then cut the mortises.

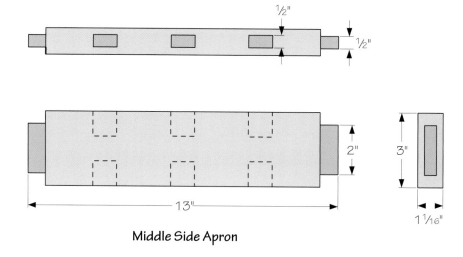

Middle Side Apron

4 Now, cut out the stringers (see drawing on proceeding page) and cut the tenons to fit the mortises in the aprons.

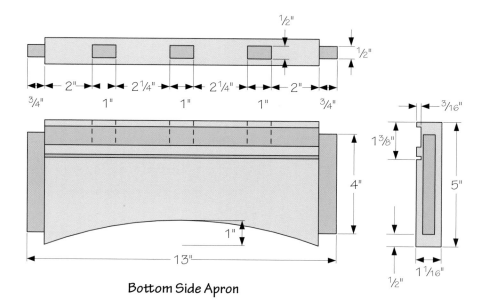

Bottom Side Apron

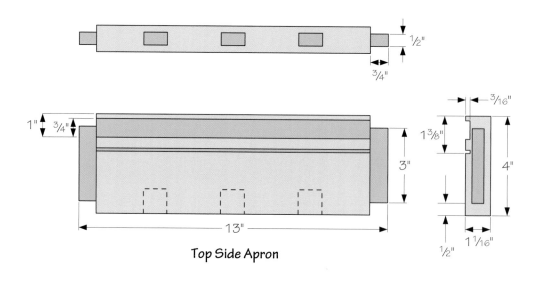

Top Side Apron

5 Before cutting out the shelves, dry assemble the cabinet, which includes the legs, all aprons and stringers. Then check the measurements for the shelves. Cut out the shelves, measure and mark the notches and cut them out.

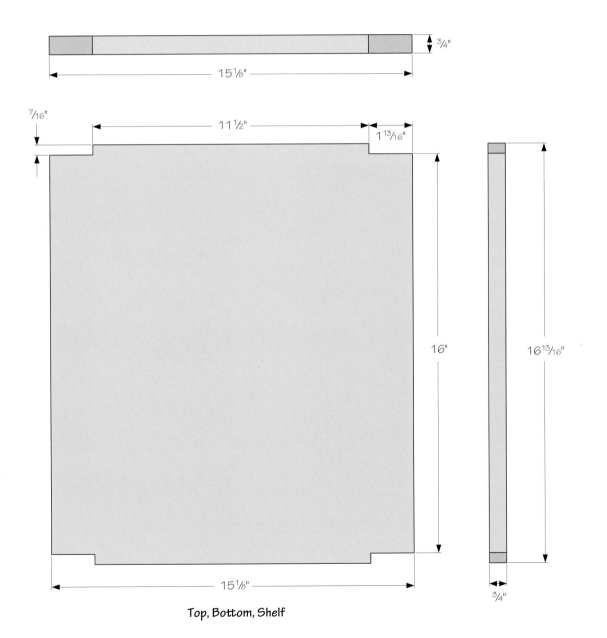

Top, Bottom, Shelf

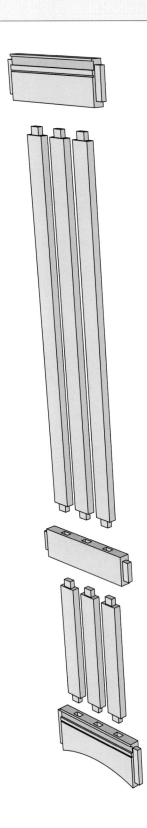

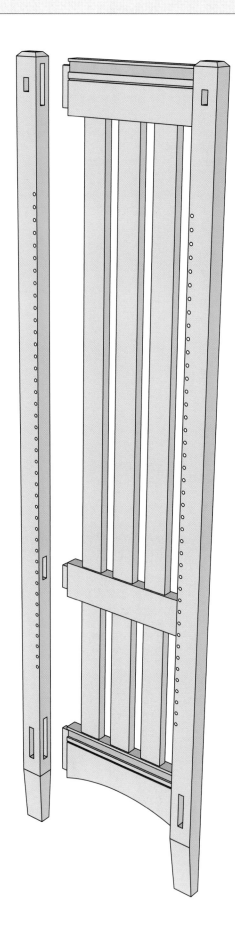

6 Once the shelves have been fitted, assemble the top and bottom stringer subassemblies. Then attach these to the legs.

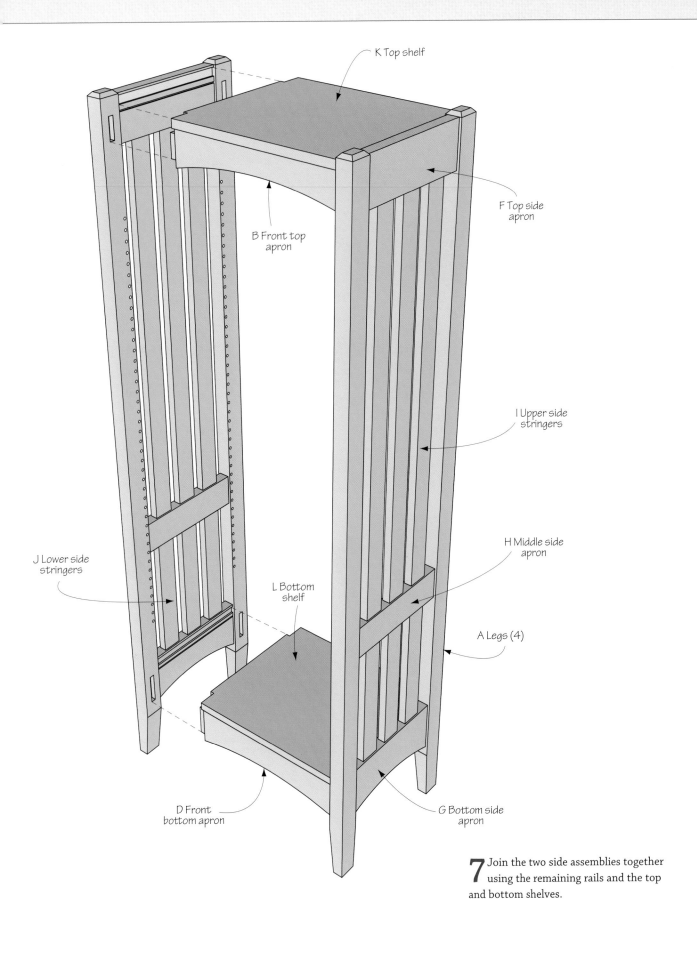

K Top shelf

F Top side
apron

B Front top
apron

I Upper side
stringers

J Lower side
stringers

H Middle side
apron

L Bottom
shelf

A Legs (4)

D Front
bottom apron

G Bottom side
apron

7 Join the two side assemblies together using the remaining rails and the top and bottom shelves.

TILE-TOP SIDE TABLE

Tile-top tables, similar to this project, have been around since the days of Gustav Stickley, and probably into the late 1800s. As a matter of fact, Gustav Stickley had an original, that, in recent years, sold for over $53,000. This truly amazed me! Early on, the tiles were hand made and could vary in color and finish.

Today, tiles are massed produced and the color and textures are relatively consistent. The design of this table combines the beauty of cherry wood with a contrasting top of ceramic tiles.

inches (millimeters)

REFERENCE	QUANTITY	PART	STOCK	THICKNESS	(mm)	WIDTH	(mm)	LENGTH	(mm)	COMMENTS
A	2	top stiles	hardwood	$1^{1}/_{16}$	(27)	$3^{5}/_{8}$	(92)	20	(508)	
B	2	top rails	hardwood	$1^{1}/_{16}$	(27)	$3^{5}/_{8}$	(92)	$18^{7}/_{16}$	(468)	
C	2	top end aprons	hardwood	$1^{1}/_{16}$	(27)	3	(76)	16	(406)	
D	2	top side aprons	hardwood	$1^{1}/_{16}$	(27)	3	(76)	$20^{3}/_{16}$	(513)	
E	1	shelf	hardwood	$^{3}/_{4}$	(19)	12	(305)	$20^{1}/_{4}$	(514)	
F	2	shelf end boards	hardwood	$^{3}/_{4}$	(19)	3	(76)	16	(406)	
G	4	legs	hardwood	$1^{3}/_{4}$	(44)	$1^{3}/_{4}$	(44)	25	(635)	
H	1	underlayment	plywood	$^{1}/_{2}$	(13)	14	(356)	$18^{3}/_{8}$	(467)	
	10	tabletop fasteners								Woodcraft #27N10 or equivalent
	12	tiles	ceramic							

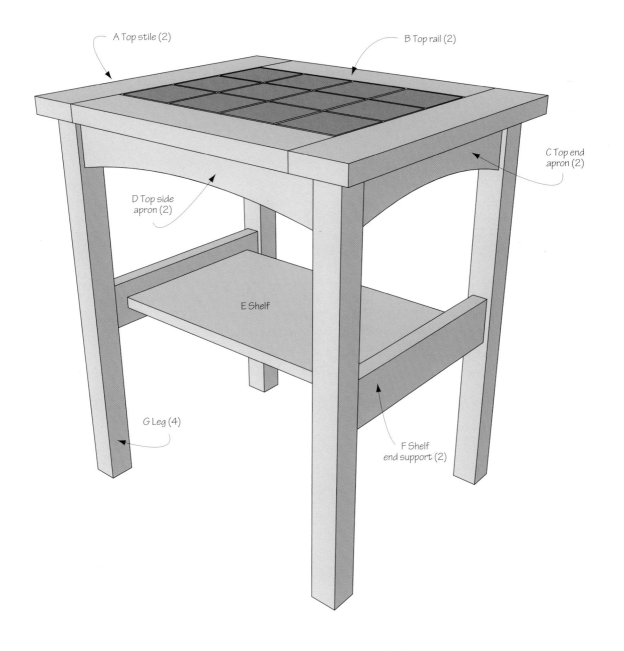

A Top stile (2)

B Top rail (2)

C Top end apron (2)

D Top side apron (2)

E Shelf

G Leg (4)

F Shelf end support (2)

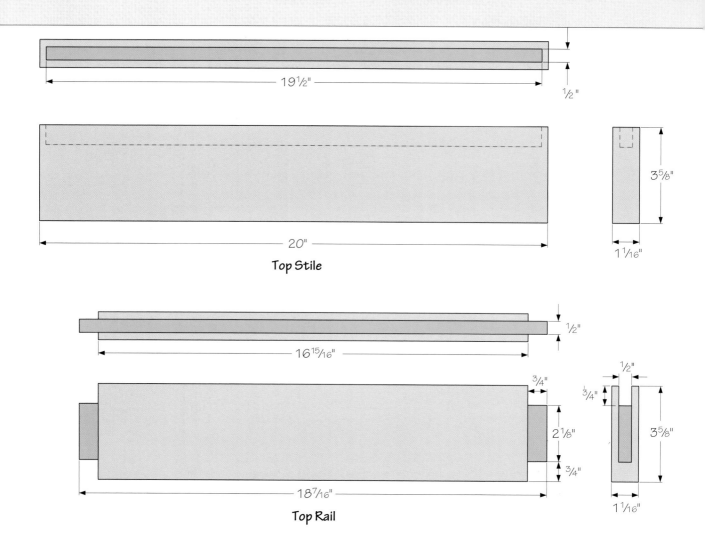

19½"

½"

3⅝"

1¹/₁₆"

Top Stile

20"

16¹⁵/₁₆"

½"

¾"

½"

¾"

2⅛"

3⅝"

¾"

18⁷/₁₆"

1¹/₁₆"

Top Rail

1 First, purchase the tiles you will be using on the top of the table. Then, lay out the tiles on a flat surface in the pattern you like. Measure the overall dimensions of the tile layout. Make adjustments to the top parts if necessary.

Now cut out the rails and stiles for the top. Cutting the grooves can be done on either a table saw with a dado blade or a router table with a ¹/₂" router bit mounted in the router. Cut through grooves in the rails and stopped grooves in the stiles. Square the ends of the stopped grooves using a chisel. Cut the tenons on the rails to fit snugly into the mortises (grooves) in the stiles.

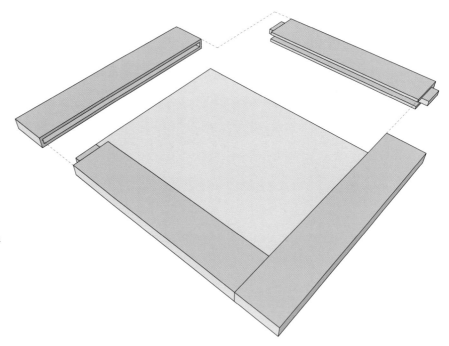

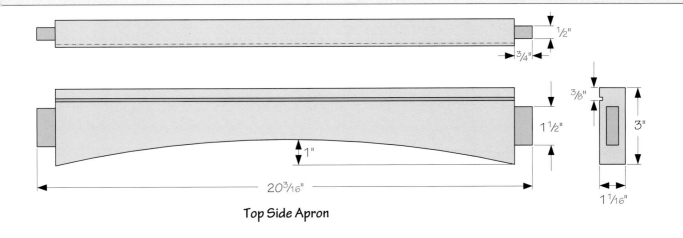

Top Side Apron

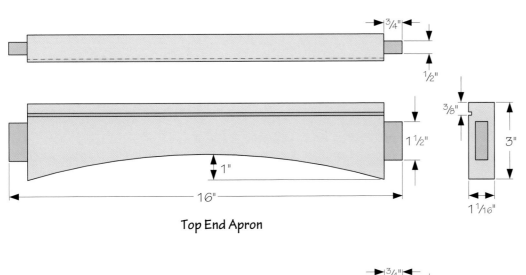

Top End Apron

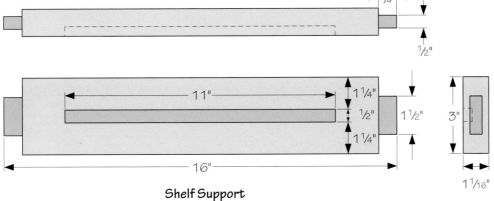

Shelf Support

2 Cut out the aprons and shelf support to size. Then cut the tenons. Lay out the mortise on the shelf supports and cut them using a router table with a ½" router bit mounted in the router or a ½" Forstener bit. Square the ends of the stopped grooves using a chisel. Cut the curves on the aprons using a band saw or jigsaw.

3 The legs have mortises cut using a $\frac{1}{2}$"
Forstner bit and a chisel or a power
mortiser.

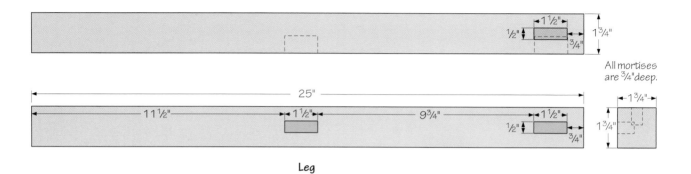

Leg

4 Cut the shelf to size. Cut the tenons
using a table saw, fitting them to the
shelf-support mortises.

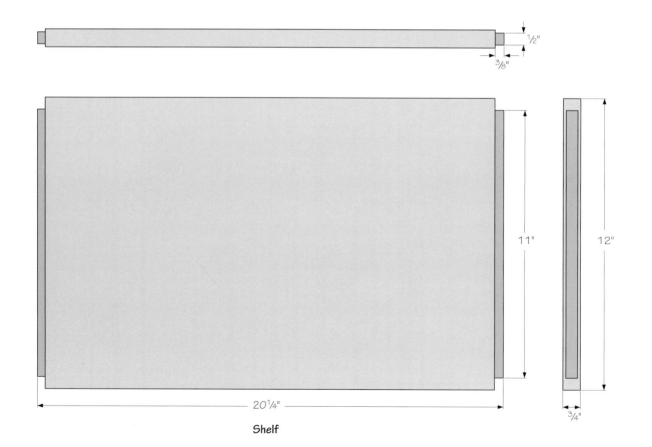

Shelf

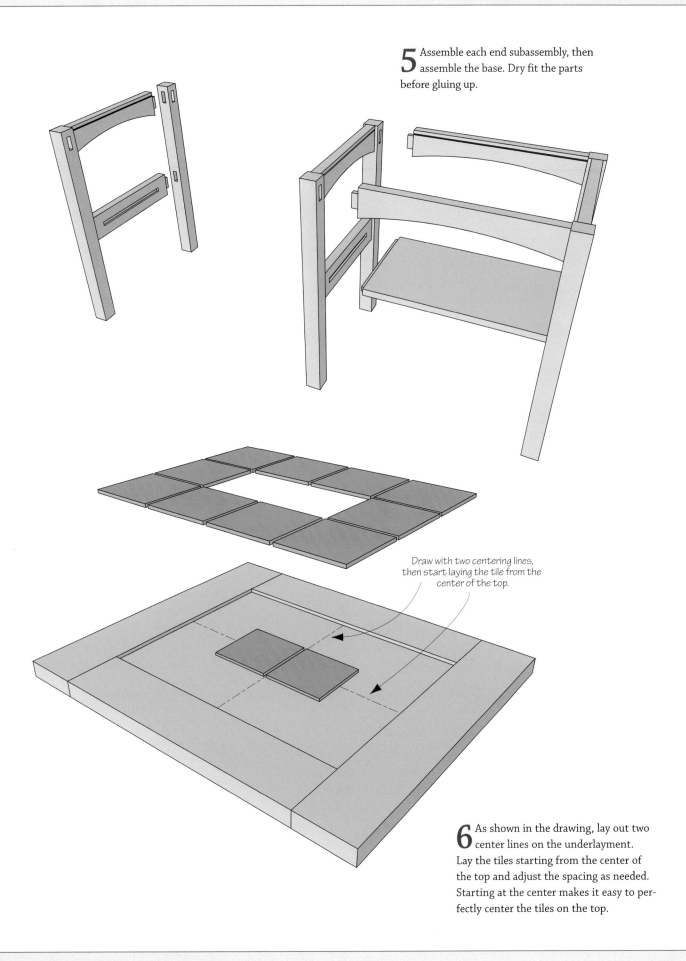

5 Assemble each end subassembly, then assemble the base. Dry fit the parts before gluing up.

Draw with two centering lines, then start laying the tile from the center of the top.

6 As shown in the drawing, lay out two center lines on the underlayment. Lay the tiles starting from the center of the top and adjust the spacing as needed. Starting at the center makes it easy to perfectly center the tiles on the top.

TILE-TOP COFFEE TABLE

Both Craftsman- and Mission-style furniture enjoyed a great deal of popularity during the late 19th and early 20th centuries. The coffee table presented here incorporates elements derived from both styles. The two features that stand out are the soft sweep of the upper aprons (the Harvey Ellis influence) and the inlaid ceramic tiles. Put together, they make for a very beautiful piece of furniture.

Made from cherry wood, with a top of twenty-eight tiles, this coffee table will find a place in any setting.

inches (millimeters)

REFERENCE	QUANTITY	PART	STOCK	THICKNESS	(mm)	WIDTH	(mm)	LENGTH	(mm)	COMMENTS
A	2	top stiles	hardwood	$1^1/_{16}$	(27)	$3^5/_8$	(92)	$24^3/_{16}$	(614)	
B	2	top rails	hardwood	$1^1/_{16}$	(27)	$3^5/_8$	(92)	32	(813)	
C	2	top end aprons	hardwood	$1^1/_{16}$	(27)	3	(76)	$35^1/_4$	(895)	
D	2	top side aprons	hardwood	$1^1/_{16}$	(27)	3	(76)	$20^3/_{16}$	(513)	
E	1	shelf	hardwood	$3/_4$	(19)	16	(406)	$35^1/_2$	(902)	
F	2	shelf end boards	hardwood	$3/_4$	(19)	3	(76)	$20^3/_{16}$	(513)	
G	4	legs	hardwood	$1^3/_4$	(44)	$1^3/_4$	(44)	16	(406)	
H	1	underlayment	plywood	$1/_2$	(13)	$18^3/_8$	(467)	$31^7/_8$	(810)	
	14	tabletop fasteners								Woodcraft #27N10 or equivalent
	28	tiles	ceramic							

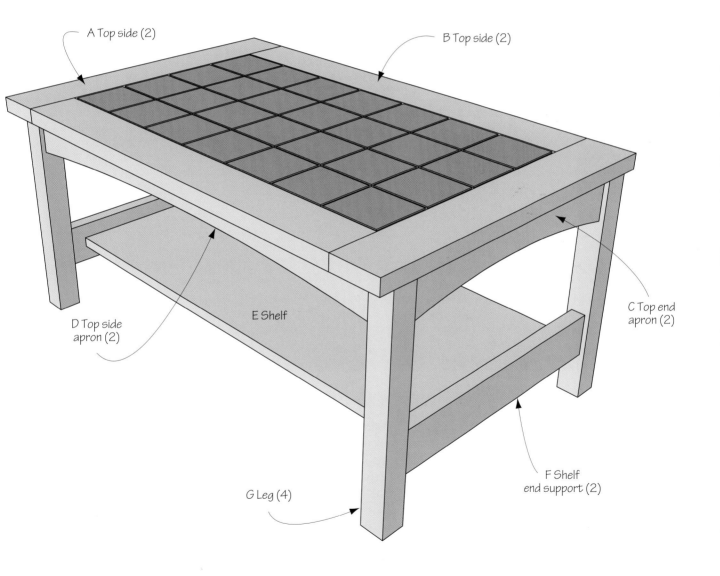

A Top side (2)

B Top side (2)

D Top side apron (2)

E Shelf

C Top end apron (2)

F Shelf end support (2)

G Leg (4)

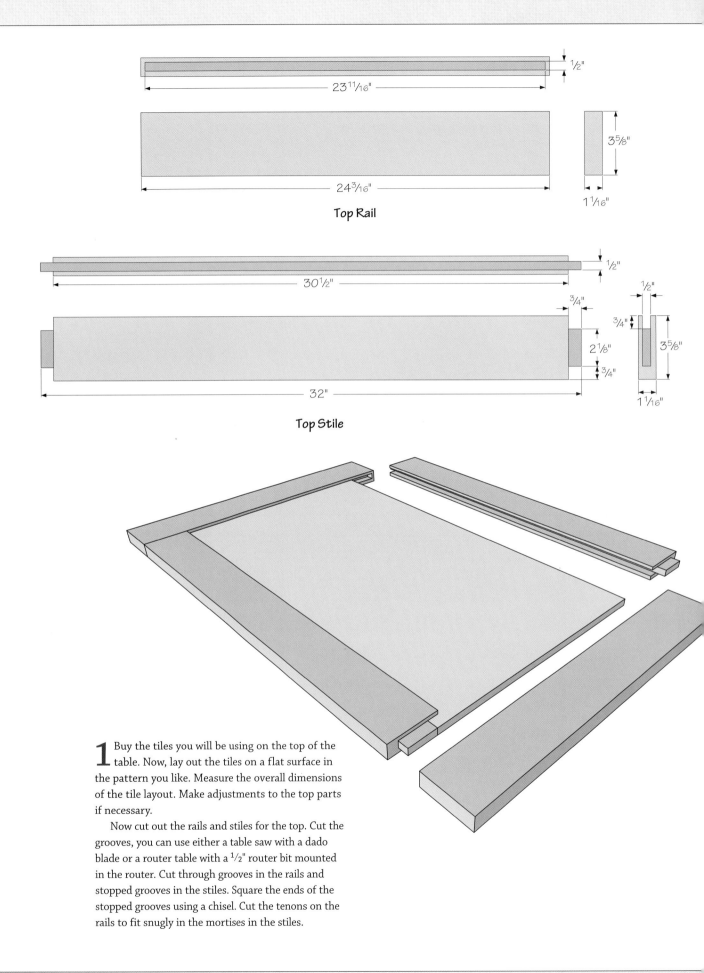

Top Rail

23¹¹⁄₁₆"

½"

3⁵⁄₈"

24³⁄₁₆"

1¹⁄₁₆"

Top Stile

30½"

½"

¾"

2¹⁄₈"

¾"

32"

½"

¾"

¾"

3⁵⁄₈"

1¹⁄₁₆"

1 Buy the tiles you will be using on the top of the table. Now, lay out the tiles on a flat surface in the pattern you like. Measure the overall dimensions of the tile layout. Make adjustments to the top parts if necessary.

Now cut out the rails and stiles for the top. Cut the grooves, you can use either a table saw with a dado blade or a router table with a ¹⁄₂" router bit mounted in the router. Cut through grooves in the rails and stopped grooves in the stiles. Square the ends of the stopped grooves using a chisel. Cut the tenons on the rails to fit snugly in the mortises in the stiles.

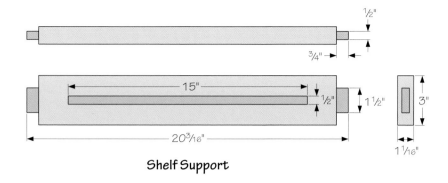

Shelf Support

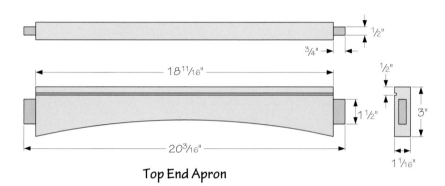

Top End Apron

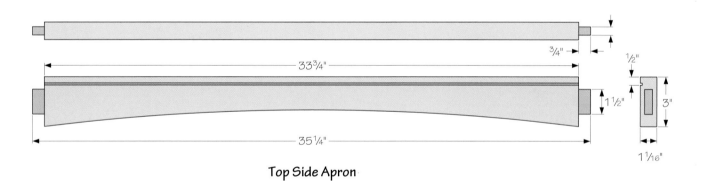

Top Side Apron

2 Cut out the aprons and shelf supports to size. Then cut the tenons. Lay out the mortise on the shelf support and cut it using a router table with a ½" router bit mounted in the router. Square the ends of the stopped grooves using a chisel. Cut the curves on the aprons using a band saw or jigsaw.

3 The legs have mortises cut using a $\frac{1}{2}$"
Forstner bit and a chisel or a power
mortiser.

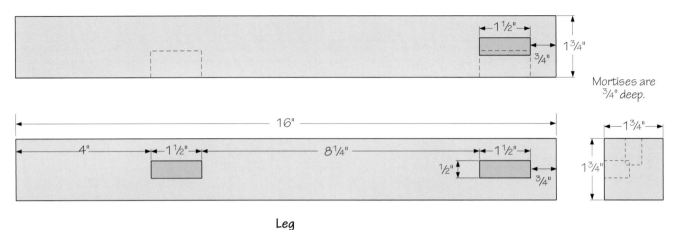

1½"

1¾"

¾"

Mortises are
¾" deep.

16"

4"   1½"   8¼"   1½"

½"   ¾"

1¾"

1¾"

Leg

4 Cut the shelf to size. Cut the tenons
using a table saw, fitting them to the
shelf-support mortises.

½"

⅜"

15"   16"

35³⁄₁₆"   ¾"

Shelf

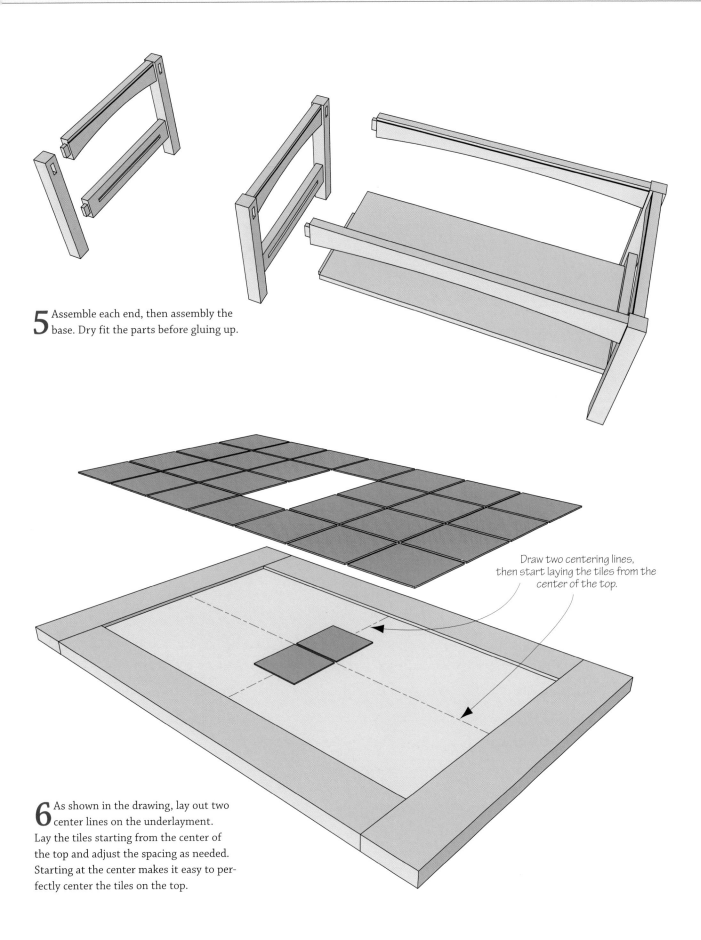

5 Assemble each end, then assembly the base. Dry fit the parts before gluing up.

Draw two centering lines, then start laying the tiles from the center of the top.

6 As shown in the drawing, lay out two center lines on the underlayment. Lay the tiles starting from the center of the top and adjust the spacing as needed. Starting at the center makes it easy to perfectly center the tiles on the top.

ONE-DRAWER BEDSIDE TABLE

I built two of these tables to sit beside an Arts & Crafts queen-sized bed. This table features a drawer to hold small stuff that is usually accumulated and has to be stored, and, an adjustable shelf to hold books. This bedside table was designed in the Arts & Crafts style, as is evidenced by the soft curves on the drawer and lower apron bottoms.

The table is made of cherry and given a slight stain, enough to simulate aging cherry. If you prefer, you can leave the cherry unstained and apply finish coats of tung oil. After a few months the cherry will darken to its own natural beauty.

inches (millimeters)

REFERENCE	QUANTITY	PART	STOCK	THICKNESS	(mm)	WIDTH	(mm)	LENGTH	(mm)	COMMENTS
A	1	top	hardwood	$3/4$	(19)	14	(356)	24	(610)	
B	1	bottom shelf	hardwood	$3/4$	(19)	$11^3/8$	(289)	$19^7/8$	(505)	cut to fit
C	1	adjustable shelf	hardwood	$3/4$	(19)	$11^1/4$	(286)	$19^{11}/16$	(500)	cut to fit
D	4	legs	hardwood	$1^3/4$	(44)	2	(51)	$27^1/4$	(692)	
E	12	stringers	hardwood	$3/4$	(19)	2	(51)	$12^1/4$	(311)	
F	1	bottom front apron	hardwood	$1^1/16$	(27)	5	(127)	20	(508)	
G	2	bottom side aprons	hardwood	$1^1/16$	(27)	6	(152)	$10^1/2$	(267)	
H	2	top side aprons	hardwood	$1^1/16$	(27)	$4^1/2$	(114)	$10^1/2$	(267)	
I	1	top rear apron	hardwood	$1^1/16$	(27)	$4^1/2$	(114)	20	(508)	
J	1	bottom rear apron	hardwood	$1^1/16$	(27)	6	(152)	20	(508)	
K	1	drawer false front	hardwood	$3/4$	(19)	$4^1/2$	(114)	$18^3/8$	(467)	
L	2	drawer front/back	hardwood	$1/2$	(13)	$3^1/4$	(83)	$18^5/16$	(465)	
M	2	drawer sides	hardwood	$1/2$	(13)	$3^1/4$	(83)	$9^1/2$	(241)	
N	1	drawer bottom	hardwood	$1/2$	(13)	$3^1/4$	(83)	$17^{11}/16$	(449)	cut to fit
O	2	drawer guides	hardwood	$1/2$	(13)	$3/4$	(19)	$9^7/8$	(251)	
	16	table-top fasteners								Woodcraft #27N10 or equivalent
	4	shelf supports								Woodcraft #27I14 or equivalent

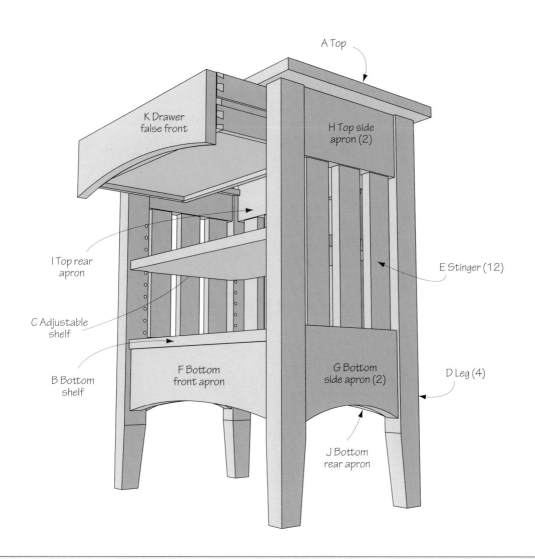

A Top

K Drawer false front

H Top side apron (2)

I Top rear apron

E Stinger (12)

C Adjustable shelf

B Bottom shelf

F Bottom front apron

G Bottom side apron (2)

D Leg (4)

J Bottom rear apron

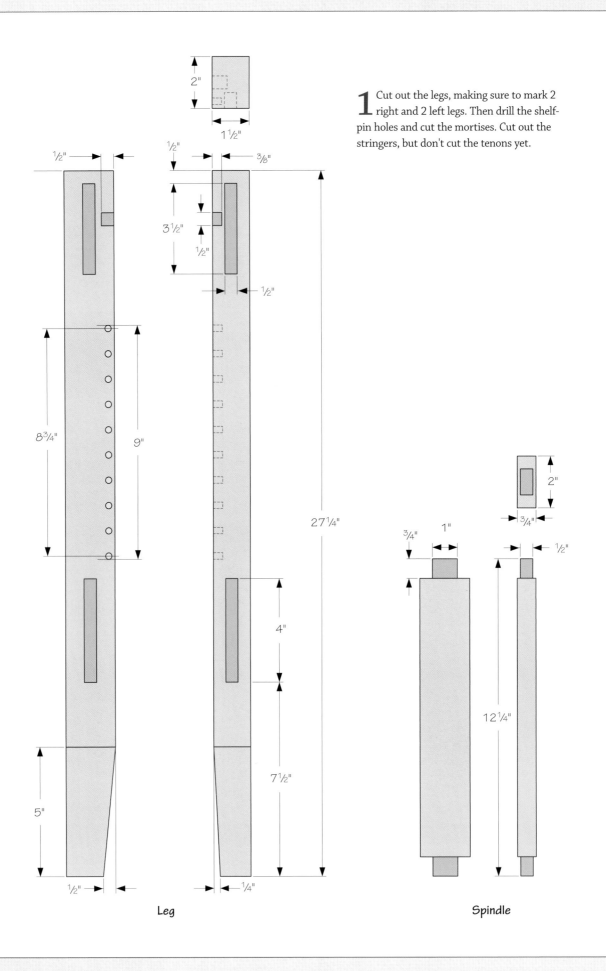

1 Cut out the legs, making sure to mark 2 right and 2 left legs. Then drill the shelf-pin holes and cut the mortises. Cut out the stringers, but don't cut the tenons yet.

Leg

Spindle

2 Cut out the top and bottom side aprons, the top and bottom rear aprons and the bottom front apron. Cut the mortises, grooves and tenons as shown. Fit the tenons to the mortises in the legs. Now you can cut the tenons on the stringers to fit the mortises in the aprons.

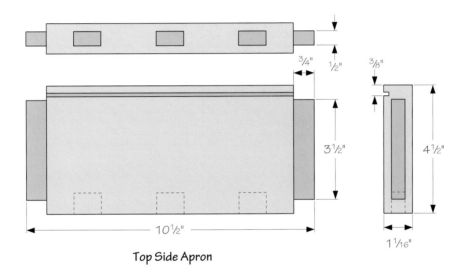

Top Side Apron

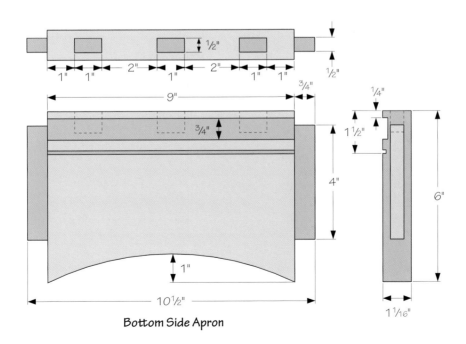

Bottom Side Apron

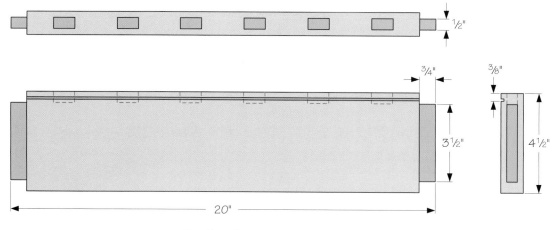

Top Rear Apron

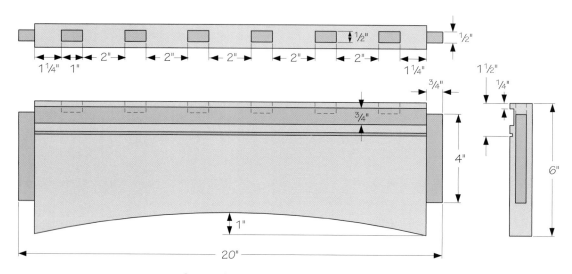

Bottom Rear Apron

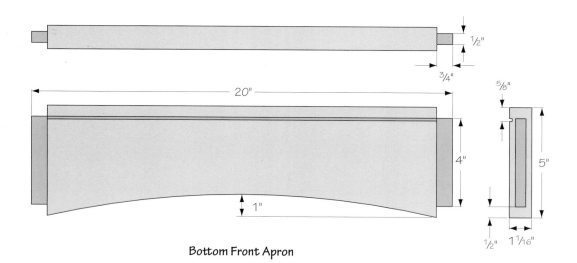

Bottom Front Apron

3 Before cutting out the bottom and adjustable shelf, dry assemble the cabinet, which includes the legs, all aprons and stringers. Then check the measurements for the shelves. Cut out the shelves, measure and mark the notches and cut them out. Cut the two drawer guides and fit them to the notches in the legs.

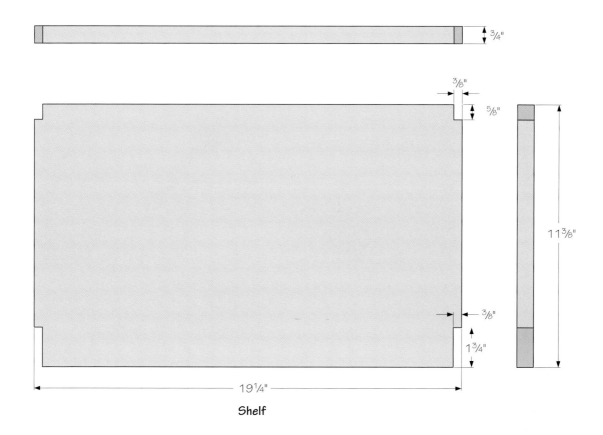

Shelf

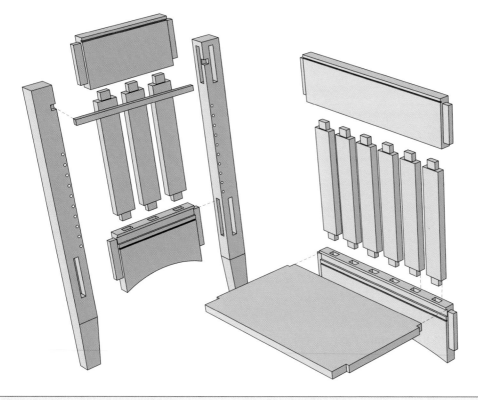

4 Glue up the two side apron-and-stringer subassemblies and the back apron-and-stringer assembly. Then, attach the legs to the side subassemblies. Join the two sides to the back subassembly and the bottom front apron. Then attach the two drawer guides.

5 Double check the measurements for the final drawer size. It can be very frustrating to cut out and assemble a drawer and not have it fit properly! Cut out the drawer front, back and sides. Cut the dovetails in the drawer parts using a router fitted with a dovetail bit. Use a dovetail jig to guide the router. Cut the grooves for the drawer bottom and the grooves for the drawer guides using a table saw or router table. Slide each side on its appropriate drawer guide. It should slide smoothly, but not too loosely.

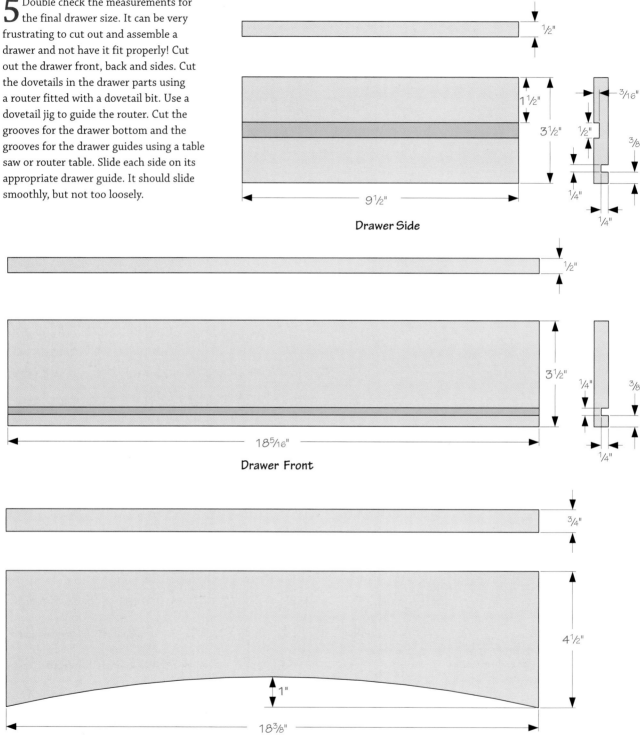

Drawer Side

Drawer Front

Drawer False Front

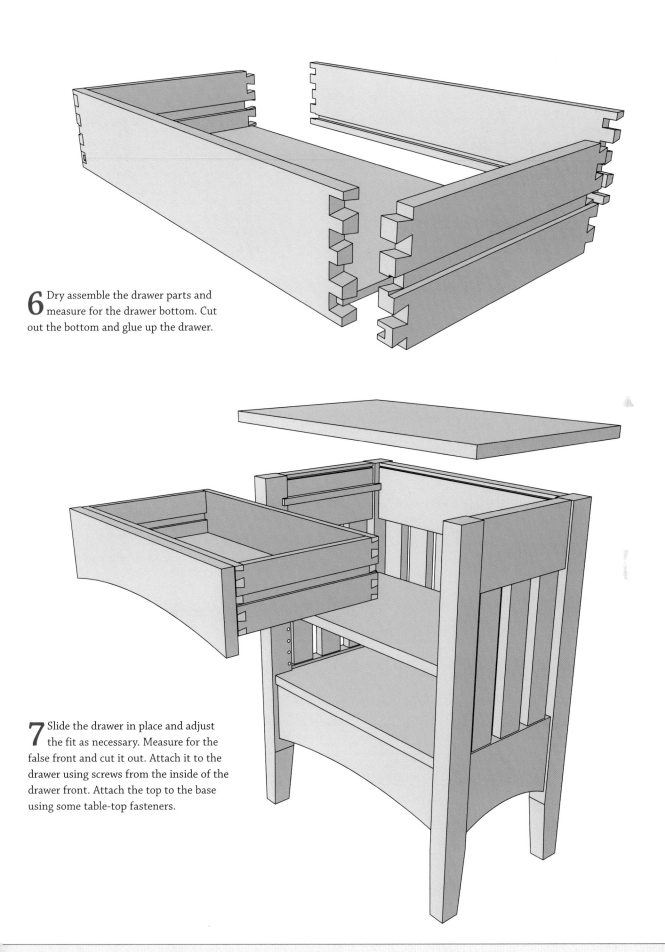

6 Dry assemble the drawer parts and measure for the drawer bottom. Cut out the bottom and glue up the drawer.

7 Slide the drawer in place and adjust the fit as necessary. Measure for the false front and cut it out. Attach it to the drawer using screws from the inside of the drawer front. Attach the top to the base using some table-top fasteners.

WINE TABLE WITH GLASS HOLDERS

Sitting next to a couple of easy chairs, this little wine table puts the wine at your finger tips; whether you're relaxing and having a bit of wine while watching a ball game or a movie on television. It's designed in the flavor of the Arts & Crafts style.

This table will hold twenty-four bottles of your favorite wines and twelve wine glasses. The design features a breadboard top and wooden wedges to keep the bottle holders in place. Many woods, such as oak, cherry or pine can be used to construct this wine table. I used my favorite wood, cherry, to construct this project.

inches (millimeters)

REFERENCE	QUANTITY	PART	STOCK	THICKNESS	(mm)	WIDTH	(mm)	LENGTH	(mm)	COMMENTS
A	1	top	hardwood	¾	(19)	16	(406)	28	(711)	
B	2	top cleats	hardwood	1½	(38)	2	(51)	12	(304)	each cleat requires 2 pieces (see illustration)
C	4	legs	hardwood	¾	(19)	2	(51)	39	(991)	
D	2	feet	hardwood	1½	(38)	2½	(64)	14	(356)	each foot requires 2 pieces (see illustration)
E	8	bottle holders	hardwood	¾	(19)	2½	(64)	25³⁄₈	(645)	
F	16	wedges	hardwood	¼	(6)	¾	(19)	2	(51)	
G	6	glass-holder cleats	hardwood	¾	(19)	1½	(38)	14	(356)	make 3 right hand and 3 left hand to form 3 sets
H	6	glass-stops	hardwood	½	(13)	1	(25)	1	(25)	
	6	wooden dowels	hardwood	¼	(6)	1	(25)			
	8	wooden dowels	hardwood	³⁄₈	(9.5)	1½	(38)			

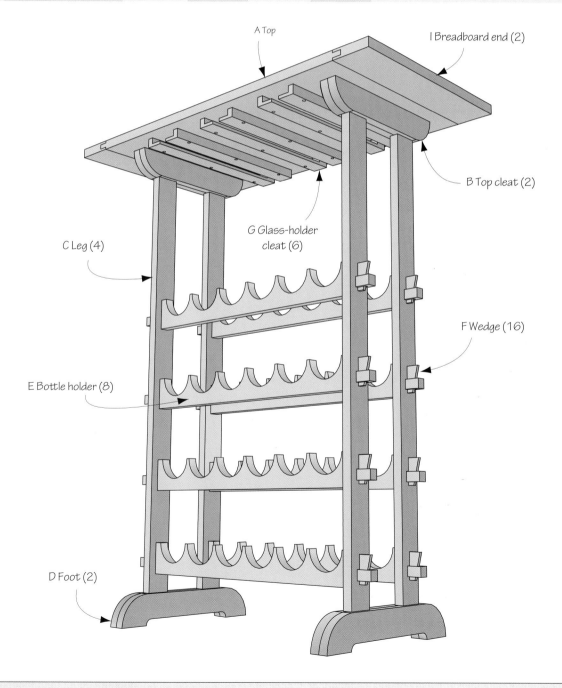

A Top

I Breadboard end (2)

B Top cleat (2)

G Glass-holder cleat (6)

C Leg (4)

F Wedge (16)

E Bottle holder (8)

D Foot (2)

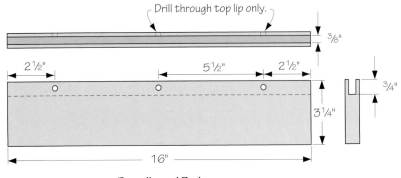

Breadboard End

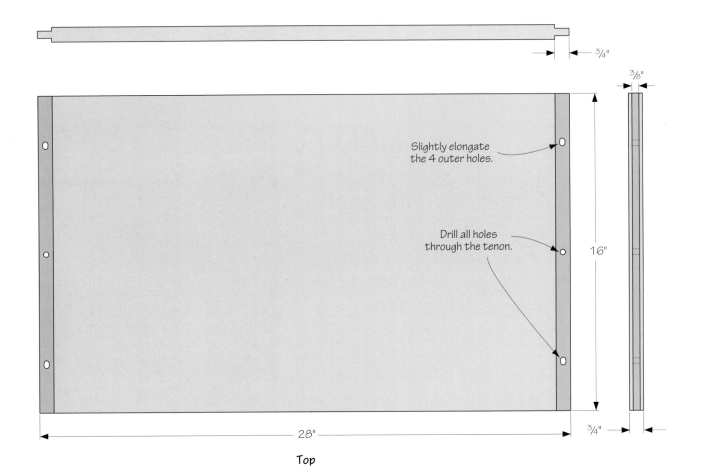

Slightly elongate the 4 outer holes.

Drill all holes through the tenon.

Top

1 Cut out the top and breadboard ends. Cut the grooves in the breadboard ends using a table saw or router table. Now, cut the tenons on the ends of the top, fitting them to the grooves in the breadboard ends. The breadboard ends should slide snugly over the tenons. Not too tight!

Drill the holes for the dowels as shown. Elongate the outside holes in the top's tenons. This will allow the top to move with the seasons and still hold the breadboard ends in place. Add glue to the center dowels and drive them into the holes. Add glue to the TOP PART of the outside dowels and drive them in place.

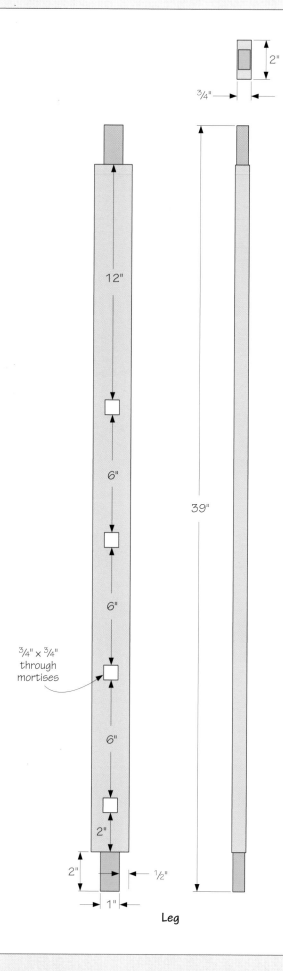

2"

¾"

2 Cut the leg blanks to size. Cut the mortises and tenons. Use a ¾" Forstner bit to drill the holes for the mortises and use a chisel to square up the corners of the mortises.

Cut out the bottle holder blanks. See the illustration for layout details. Fit the tenons to the mortises in the legs. Put the tenons through the mortises in the legs to mark the locations of the tapered mortises. Then cut these mortises.

12"

6"

39"

6"

¾" × ¾"
through
mortises

6"

2"

2"   ½"

1"

Leg

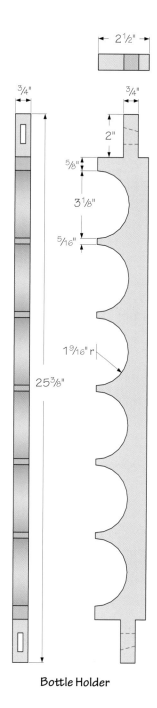

2½"

¾"   ¾"

2"

⅝"

3⅛"

⁵⁄₁₆"

1⁹⁄₁₆" r

25⅜"

Bottle Holder

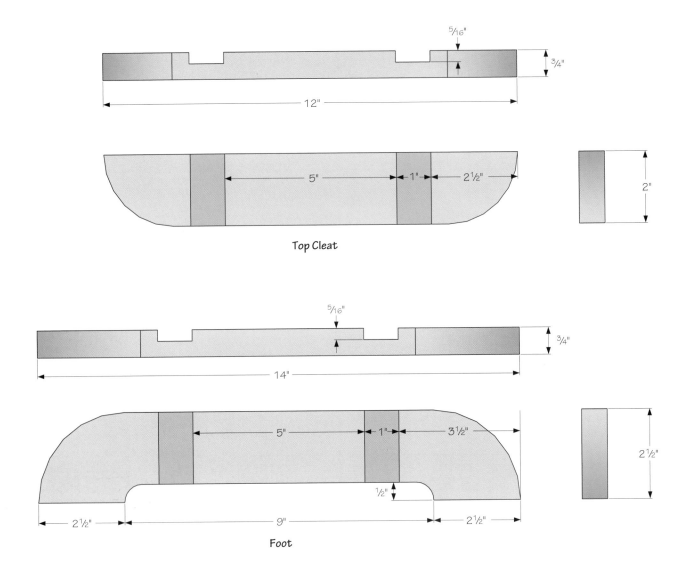

Top Cleat

Foot

3 The feet and cleats are made with two parts each. The illustration shows the layout. Cut the dadoes first. When cutting the dadoes, fit them to the tenons on the legs. To ensure that pairs of parts are the same, use double-stick tape to hold them together. Cut and sand the radii on the top cleats. Also cut the radii on the feet and the clearance cutouts to create the feet.

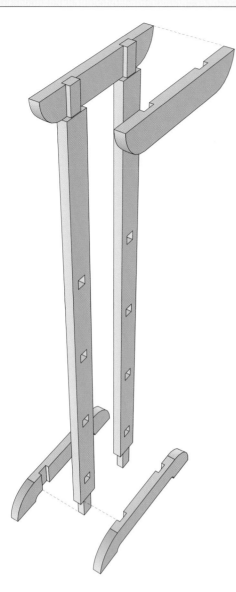

4 Separate the cleat and foot parts and glue up the leg subassemblies.

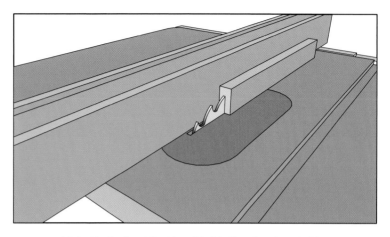

Make the first cut for the rabbet in the wine glass-holder cleats by running the part on edge.

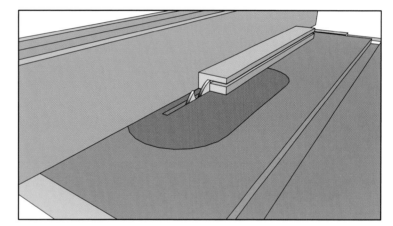

Make the second cut for the rabbet in the wine glass-holder cleats ++by running the part on its face.

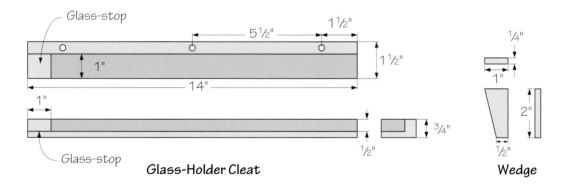

Glass-stop

1 1/2"

5 1/2"

1"

1 1/2"

14"

1"

3/4"

1/2"

Glass-stop

Glass-Holder Cleat

1/4"

1"

2"

1/2"

Wedge

5 Cut out the glass-holder blanks. Cut the rabbits using a table saw using a single blade. See the above illustrations. Set the fence ¼" from the blade and set the blade 1" high and make the first cut. Then set the fence ½" from the blade and set the blade ½" high and make the second. Cut out the glass-stop parts and glue them in place as shown. Be sure to make 3 right-handed and 3 left-handed parts. Drill the mounting holes. Cut the wedges and fit them into the mortises that are located in the tenons on the bottle holders.

6 Starting with one leg assembly, insert the bottle holders into the mortises and install the wedges. Lay this assembly on its side with the bottle holders sticking up. Install the other leg assembly and insert the wedges. The base is now assembled!

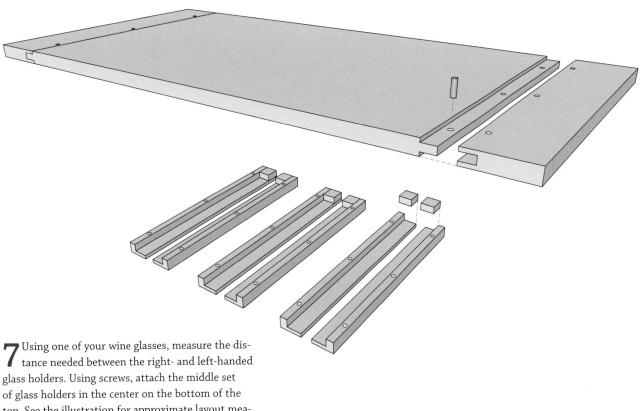

7 Using one of your wine glasses, measure the distance needed between the right- and left-handed glass holders. Using screws, attach the middle set of glass holders in the center on the bottom of the top. See the illustration for approximate layout measurements. Attach the top to the base using screws through the top cleats.

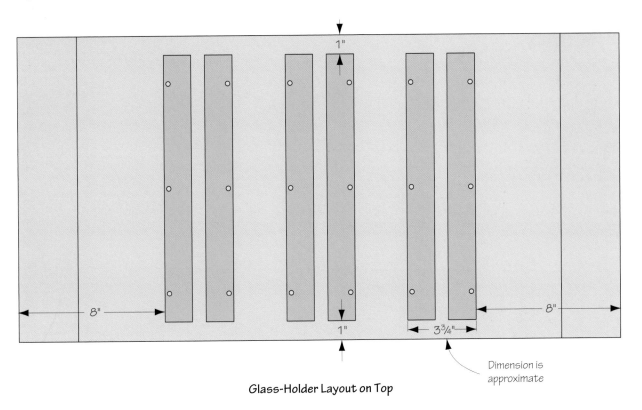

1"

1"

8"

8"

3¾"

Dimension is
approximate

Glass-Holder Layout on Top

WINE CABINET

This beautiful Mission-styled wine cabinet will hold 30 bottles of wine. There is also a drawer that can hold bottle openers, stoppers and all the other things that you need when serving wine.

inches (millimeters)

REFERENCE	QUANTITY	PART	STOCK	THICKNESS	(mm)	WIDTH	(mm)	LENGTH	(mm)	COMMENTS
A	1	top	hardwood	$3/4$	(19)	$16^{1}/4$	(413)	$29^{1}/2$	(749)	
B	1	top backsplash	hardwood	$3/4$	(19)	$2^{1}/2$	(64)	28	(711)	
C	2	bottom side aprons	hardwood	$3/4$	(19)	$4^{5}/8$	(117)	$16^{1}/4$	(813)	cut to fit
D	1	bottom front apron	hardwood	$3/4$	(19)	$4^{5}/8$	(117)	$29^{1}/2$	(749)	cut to fit
E	4	side stiles	hardwood	$3/4$	(19)	$2^{1}/2$	(64)	$32^{3}/4$	(832)	
F	2	top side rails	hardwood	$3/4$	(19)	$3^{1}/4$	(83)	$12^{1}/2$	(318)	
G	2	bottom side rails	hardwood	$3/4$	(19)	$6^{1}/4$	(159)	$12^{1}/2$	(318)	
H	4	side panels	plywood	$1/2$	(13)	$11^{1}/2$	(292)	$24^{1}/4$	(616)	each panel made of 2, $1/4$- panels, glued good faces out
I	2	side top trim	hardwood	$5/8$	(16)	$5/8$	(16)	$16^{1}/4$	(813)	cut to fit
J	1	front top trim	hardwood	$5/8$	(16)	$5/8$	(16)	$29^{1}/2$	(749)	cut to fit
K	1	back	plywood	$1/4$	(6)	$27^{1}/4$	(692)	$33^{1}/2$	(851)	cut to fit
L	1	top front rail	hardwood	$3/4$	(19)	$1^{1}/2$	(38)	$26^{1}/2$	(673)	
M	1	bottom front rail	hardwood	$3/4$	(19)	$3^{7}/8$	(98)	$26^{1}/2$	(673)	
N	1	top back rail	hardwood	$3/4$	(19)	4	(102)	$26^{1}/2$	(673)	
O	1	bottom back rail	hardwood	$1^{3}/4$	(44)	$6^{1}/4$	(159)	$26^{1}/2$	(673)	
P	1	front bottom drawer support	hardwood	$3/4$	(19)	2	(51)	$26^{1}/2$	(673)	
Q	1	rear bottom drawer support	hardwood	$3/4$	(19)	2	(51)	$26^{1}/2$	(673)	
R	2	side drawer supports	hardwood	$1^{1}/16$	(27)	$3^{5}/8$	(92)	$12^{1}/8$	(308)	
S	1	drawer support dust shield	plywood	$1/4$	(6)	$11^{1}/8$	(238)	$23^{1}/2$	(570)	
T	1	cabinet bottom	plywood	$3/4$	(19)	$11^{13}/16$	(300)	$26^{7}/8$	(683)	
U	1	cabinet bottom front	hardwood	$3/4$	(19)	$2^{1}/2$	(64)	$26^{1}/2$	(673)	
V	8	bottle-shelf rails	hardwood	$3/4$	(19)	2	(51)	25	(635)	
W	8	bottle-shelf stiles	hardwood	$3/4$	(19)	2	(51)	11	(279)	
X	35	bottle-shelf partitions	hardwood	$3/4$	(19)	$1^{1}/4$	(32)	13	(330)	
Y	4	bottle-shelf dust shield	plywood	$1/4$	(6)	11	(279)	$21^{1}/2$	(546)	
Z	1	false drawer front	hardwood	$3/4$	(19)	4	(102)	$26^{1}/2$	(673)	
AA	4	door stiles	hardwood	$3/4$	(19)	2	(51)	$21^{3}/4$	(552)	
AB	4	door rails	hardwood	$3/4$	(19)	2	(51)	$10^{5}/8$	(270)	
AC	2	drawer front/back	hardwood	$1/2$	(13)	3	(76)	$25^{1}/2$	(648)	
AD	2	drawer sides	hardwood	$1/2$	(13)	3	(76)	12	(305)	
AE	4	shelf-slide shims	hardwood	$5/16$	(8)	$1^{1}/2$	(38)	$21^{3}/4$	(552)	
AF	1	bottom-shelf rear support	hardwood	$1/2$	(13)	$1^{1}/4$	(32)	$25^{15}/16$	(659)	
AG	4	bottle-shelf rear support	hardwood	$1/2$	(13)	$1^{1}/4$	(32)	25	(635)	
AH	1	drawer bottom	plywood	$1/4$	(6)	$11^{1}/2$	(292)	25	(635)	cut to fit
AI	4	bottle-shelf pulls	hardwood	$1/2$	(13)	$1/2$	(13)	4	(102)	
AJ	8	bottle-shelf sides	hardwood	$3/4$	(19)	$1^{1}/4$	(32)	13	(330)	
AK	4	legs	hardwood	$1^{3}/4$	(44)	$1^{3}/4$	(44)	16	(406)	
AL	1	underlayment	plywood	$1/2$	(13)	$18^{3}/8$	(467)	$31^{7}/8$	(810)	

HARDWARE

Door hinges	2 pairs	Rockler #26849
Door knobs	2	Rockler #10871
Door knobs back plates	2	Rockler #10923
Drawer pulls	2	Rockler #62919
Drawer slides, 12"	1 set	local home center
Drawer slides, 14"	4 sets	local home center
Tabletop fasteners	20	Rockler #34215
Bronze glass, $\frac{1}{8}$"	2	$9\frac{7}{8} \times 17\frac{9}{16}$ (measure for glass after door is made
Taper pads, glass holders	20	Rockler #28530
Low-profile magnetic catch	1	Rockler #26542

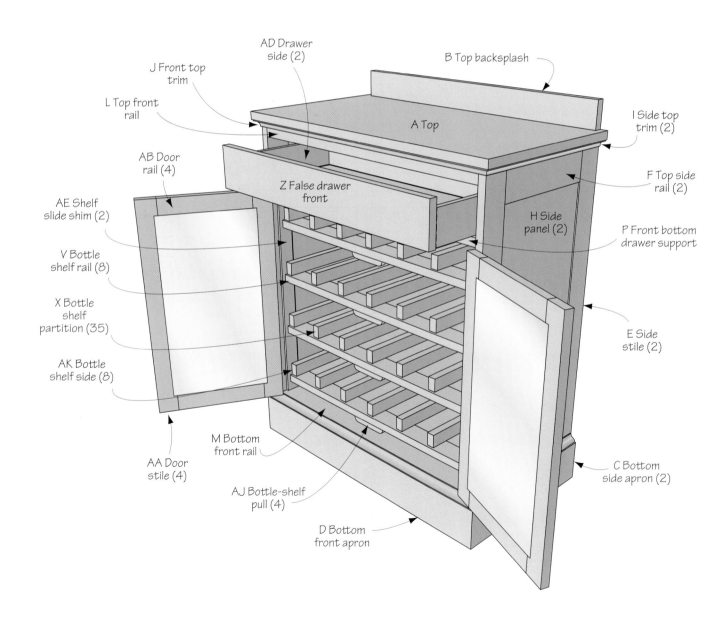

1 Cut out the side stiles and top and bottom rails. The front stiles have a groove and two mortises. The back stiles have a groove and two mortises, plus a stopped rabbit that will accept the back panel. Cut the stopped rabbit using a router table. Mark the stopped ends on the router table fence and on the back stiles. Then start the cut at the first mark on the fence and stop at the other mark. Square the corners of the stopped rabbits using a chisel. Remember to make right- and left-hand front and back side stiles. (Each stile will look different.) Dry assemble the frames and double check the dimensions of the side panels. Then cut out the panels.

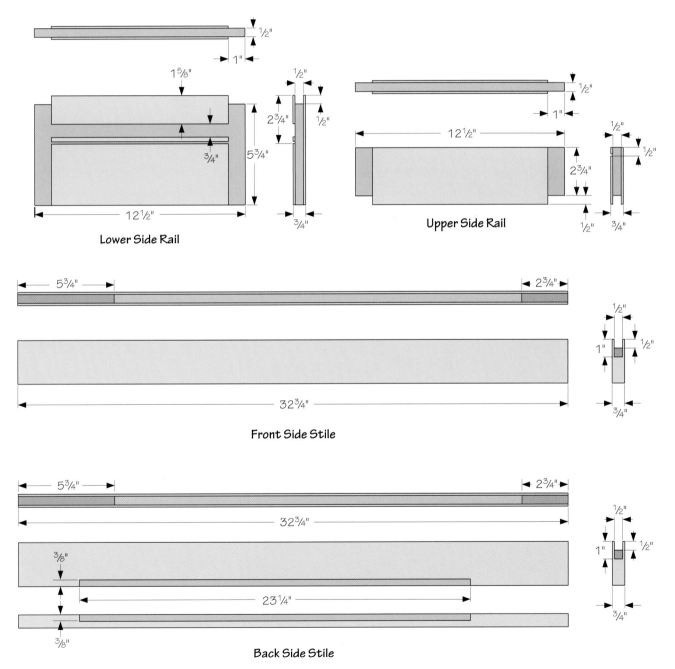

Lower Side Rail

Upper Side Rail

Front Side Stile

Back Side Stile

2 Cut the drawer-support parts to dimension. Cut the grooves, then cut the tenons on the rails to fit the grooves. Dry assemble this frame and double check the dimensions for the dust panel. Then cut out the dust panel.

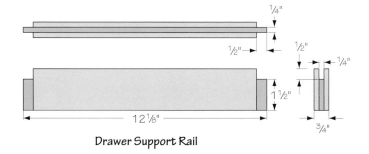

¼"

½" ½"

¼"

1½"

12⅛"

¾"

Drawer Support Rail

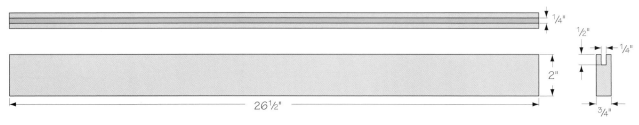

¼"

½" ¼"

2"

26½"

¾"

Drawer Support Stile

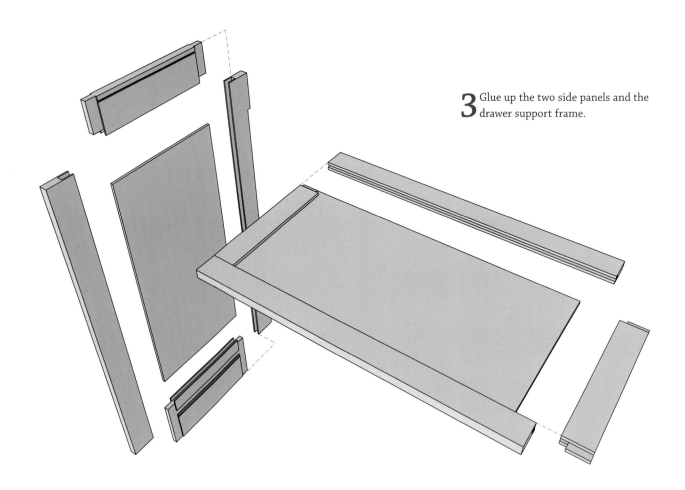

3 Glue up the two side panels and the drawer support frame.

4 Cut the top and bottom back rails and the front rail to dimension. Then cut the grooves as shown in the illustrations.

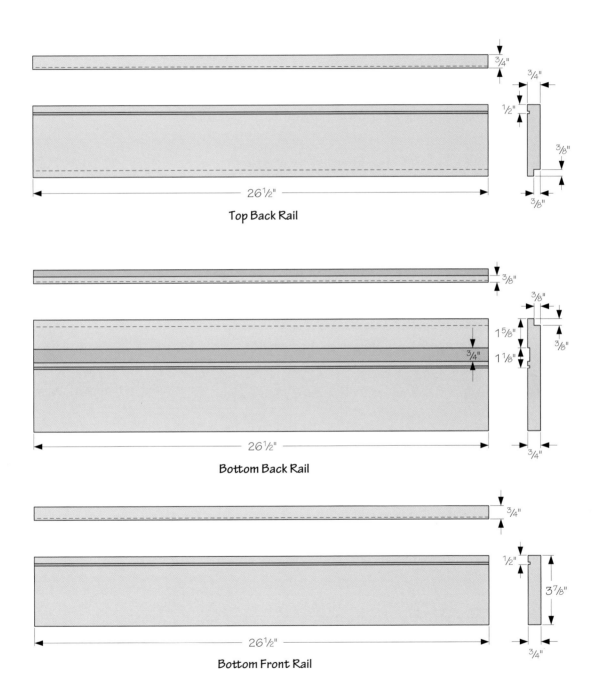

Top Back Rail

Bottom Back Rail

Bottom Front Rail

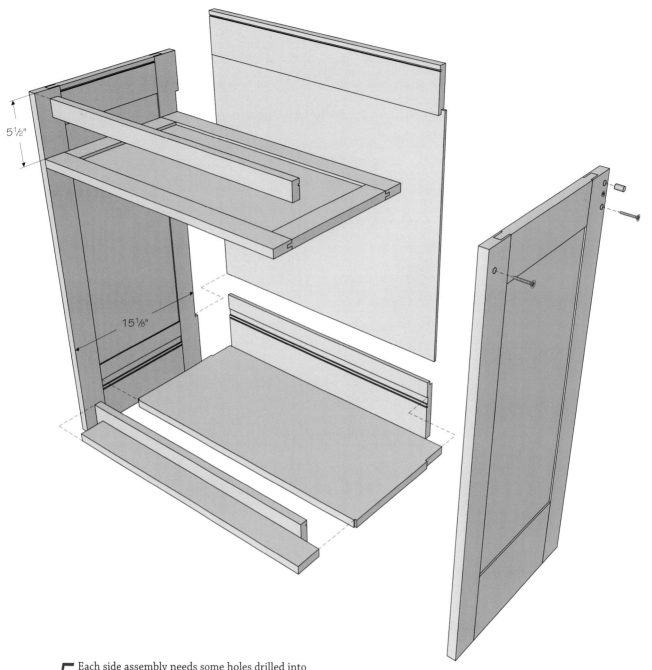

5 Each side assembly needs some holes drilled into them for the flat head wood screws that secure the other parts. Mark the location of the holes on the side subassemblies. Don't forget, one side is the mirror image of the other. After center punching each mark, use a $^3/_8$" Forstner bit to bore holes no more than a $^1/_4$" deep in each location. Now drill the $^1/_4$" clearance holes for the screws. Use wooden plugs to cover the screw heads and fill the holes.

6 Cut the drawer parts to size, then cut the dovetails using a router and a template. Now cut the groove for the bottom. The bottom is installed at the same time the drawer parts are glued together. Wait to install the drawer false front until final assembly.

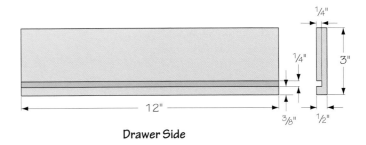

Drawer Side

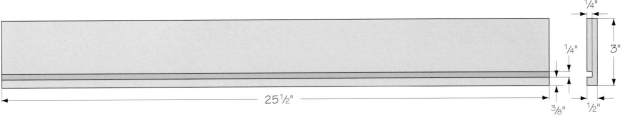

Drawer Front/Back

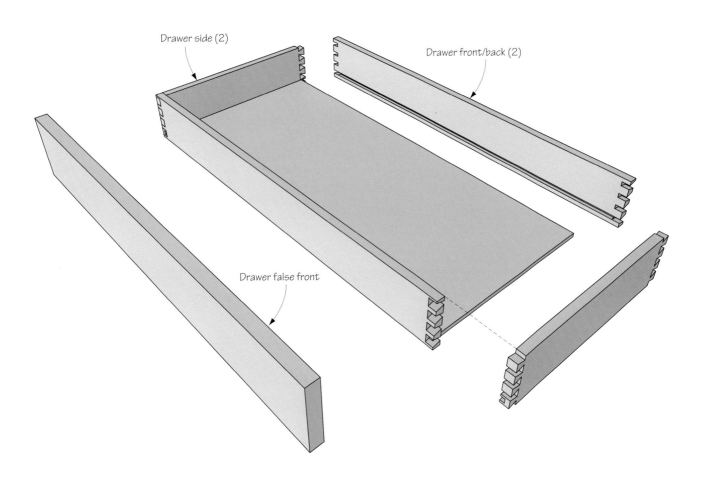

7 Cut out the bottle-shelf parts and machine them as shown in the illustration, using the techniques described throughout this book. Assemble each shelf as shown in the illustration. Attach the bottle-shelf partitions by installing screws from the bottom of each bottle-shelf rail.

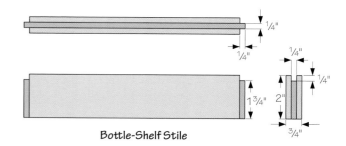

Bottle-Shelf Stile

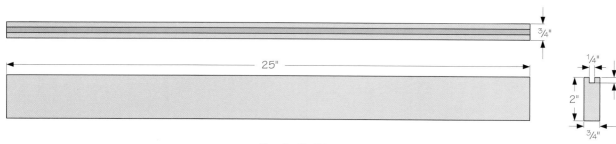

Bottle-Shelf Rail

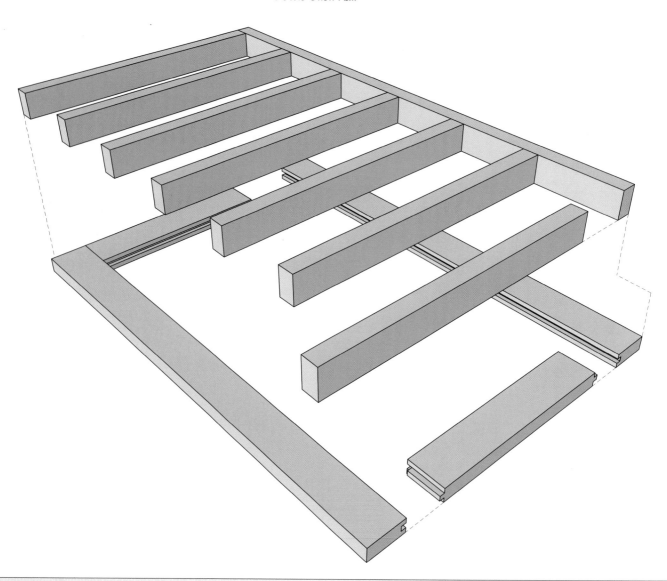

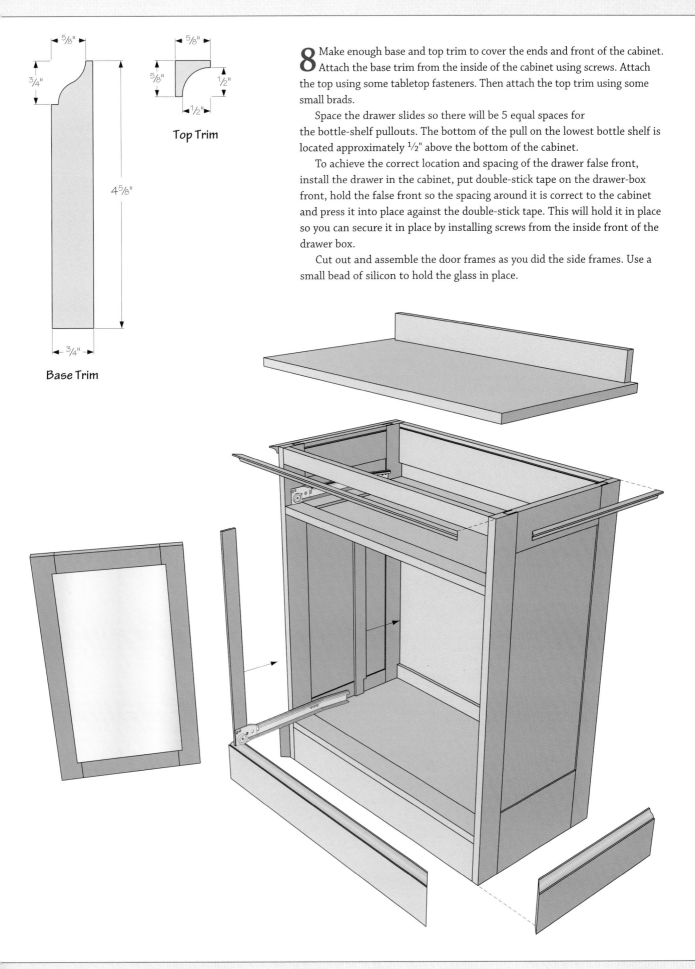

5/8"

3/4"

Top Trim

5/8"

5/8"

1/2"

1/2"

4 5/8"

3/4"

Base Trim

8 Make enough base and top trim to cover the ends and front of the cabinet. Attach the base trim from the inside of the cabinet using screws. Attach the top using some tabletop fasteners. Then attach the top trim using some small brads.

Space the drawer slides so there will be 5 equal spaces for the bottle-shelf pullouts. The bottom of the pull on the lowest bottle shelf is located approximately 1/2" above the bottom of the cabinet.

To achieve the correct location and spacing of the drawer false front, install the drawer in the cabinet, put double-stick tape on the drawer-box front, hold the false front so the spacing around it is correct to the cabinet and press it into place against the double-stick tape. This will hold it in place so you can secure it in place by installing screws from the inside front of the drawer box.

Cut out and assemble the door frames as you did the side frames. Use a small bead of silicon to hold the glass in place.

ROCKING CHAIR

What could be more relaxing than rocking in a chair on a lazy afternoon? This rocking chair is built in the tradition of a Morris chair with rockers. It's upholstered with a fabric that has a Southwestern United States pattern. This chair is made of cherry and lightly stained a cherry color, which will darken over time to a rich, deep reddish-brown color. Finish it with polyurethane or lacquer.

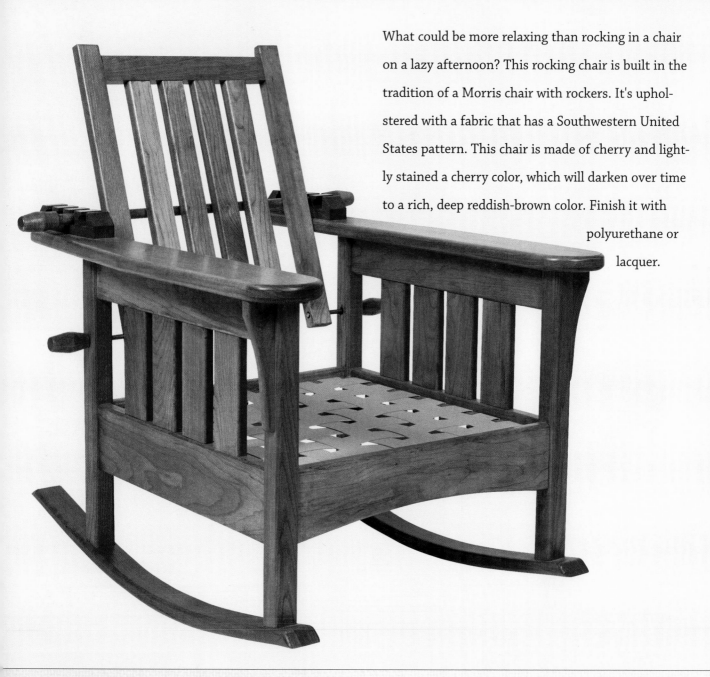

inches (millimeters)

REFERENCE	QUANTITY	PART	STOCK	THICKNESS	(mm)	WIDTH	(mm)	LENGTH	(mm)	COMMENTS
A	2	back stiles	hardwood	1¹/₁₆	(27)	2	(51)	23	(584)	
B	2	back rails	hardwood	1¹/₁₆	(27)	2	(51)	17	(432)	
C	4	back slats	hardwood	1¹/₁₆	(27)	2	(51)	18	(457)	
D	4	legs	hardwood	1³/₄	(44)	1³/₄	(44)	22	(559)	cut to fit the rockers
E	1	front apron	hardwood	1¹/₁₆	(27)	4³/₄	(121)	23¹/₂	(597)	
F	1	rear apron	hardwood	1¹/₁₆	(27)	4³/₄	(121)	23¹/₂	(597)	
G	2	upper side aprons	hardwood	1¹/₁₆	(27)	3	(76)	23¹/₂	(597)	
H	2	lower side aprons	hardwood	1¹/₁₆	(27)	4³/₄	(121)	23¹/₂	(597)	
I	8	side slats	hardwood	³/₄	(19)	3	(76)	9¹/₂	(241)	
J	2	back support brackets	hardwood	1³/₄	(44)	1³/₄	(44)	9	(229)	
K	2	arms	hardwood	1¹/₁₆	(27)	5¹/₂	(140)	36	(914)	
L	1	support rod	hardwood	³/₄ d	(19)			26¹/₄	(667)	
M	2	support-rod ends	hardwood	1¹/₂ d	(38)	2¹/₄	(57)			
N	2	pivot rods	steel	³/₈ d	(9.5)	7	(178)			
O	2	pivot-rod ends	hardwood	1¹/₂ d	(38)	2¹/₄	(57)			
P	4	webbing supports	hardwood	³/₄	(19)	1	(25)	21¹/₂	(546)	
Q	6	rockers	hardwood	³/₄	(19)	6	(152)	38	(965)	3 pieces per rocker
R	2	arm supports	hardwood	³/₄	(19)	2	(51)	8	(203)	

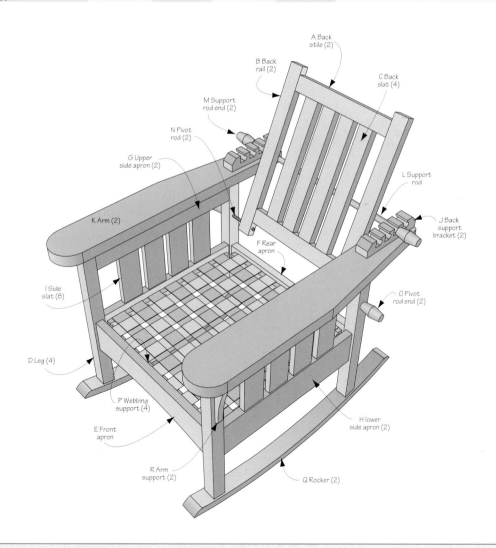

1 Cut out the leg blanks. You'll need to make 2 right and 2 left legs. Label each leg before you lay out the mortises. This will help you from making layout mistakes. Then cut the mortises and drill the holes. Use a drill press to ensure that the holes are perfectly square to the face of the legs. Don't cut the miters on the legs at this time.

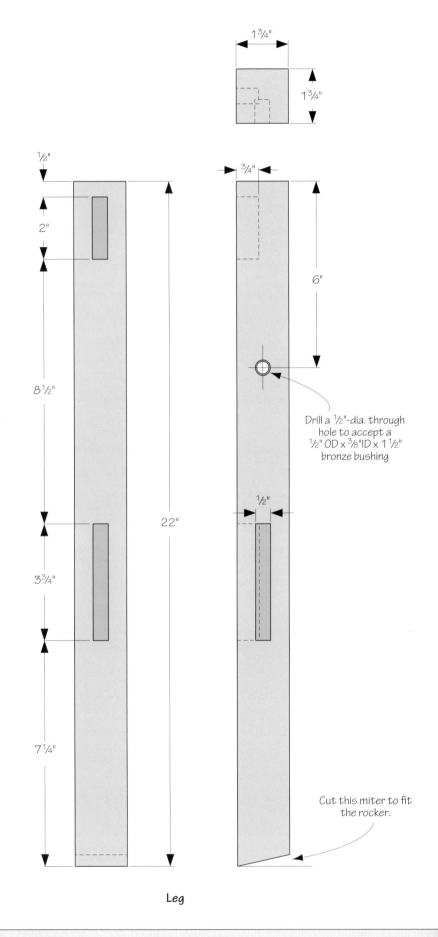

1¾"

1¾"

½"

2"

8½"

3¾"

7¼"

22"

¾"

6"

Drill a ½"-dia. through hole to accept a ½" OD x ⅜"ID x 1½" bronze bushing

½"

Cut this miter to fit the rocker.

Leg

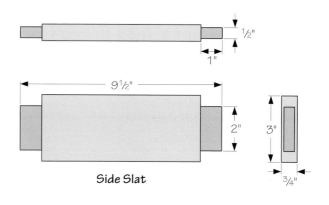

2 Cut out the parts for the side assemblies and the front and back aprons. Cut the mortises in the upper and lower side aprons first. Then cut and fit the tenons on the side slats to these mortises. Then cut and fit the tenons on the upper and lower side aprons and the front/back aprons to fit the mortises in the legs.

Side Slat

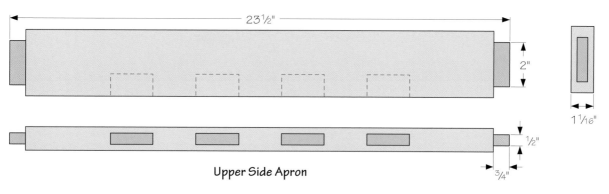

Upper Side Apron

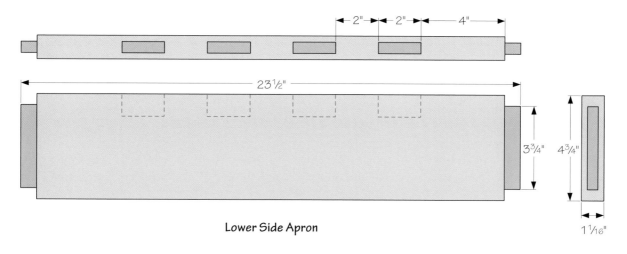

Lower Side Apron

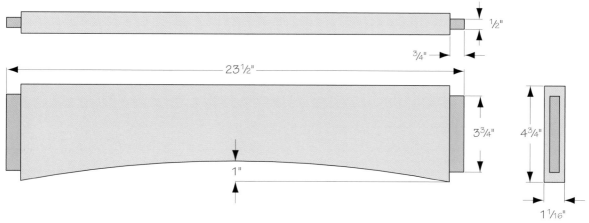

Front/Rear Apron

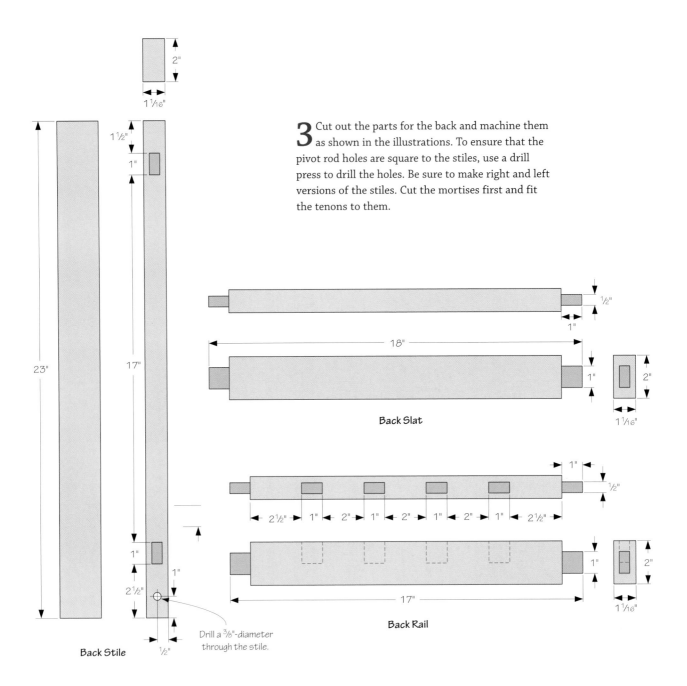

3 Cut out the parts for the back and machine them as shown in the illustrations. To ensure that the pivot rod holes are square to the stiles, use a drill press to drill the holes. Be sure to make right and left versions of the stiles. Cut the mortises first and fit the tenons to them.

2"

1 ¹/₁₆"

1 ½"

1"

23"

17"

1"

2 ½"

Drill a ³/₈"-diameter through the stile.

Back Stile

½"

½"

1"

18"

1"

1"

2"

Back Slat

1 ¹/₁₆"

1"

½"

2 ½" 1" 2" 1" 2" 1" 2" 1" 2 ½"

1"

17"

1"

2"

Back Rail

1 ¹/₁₆"

4 Dry assemble the back to ensure everything fits together properly. Then glue it together.

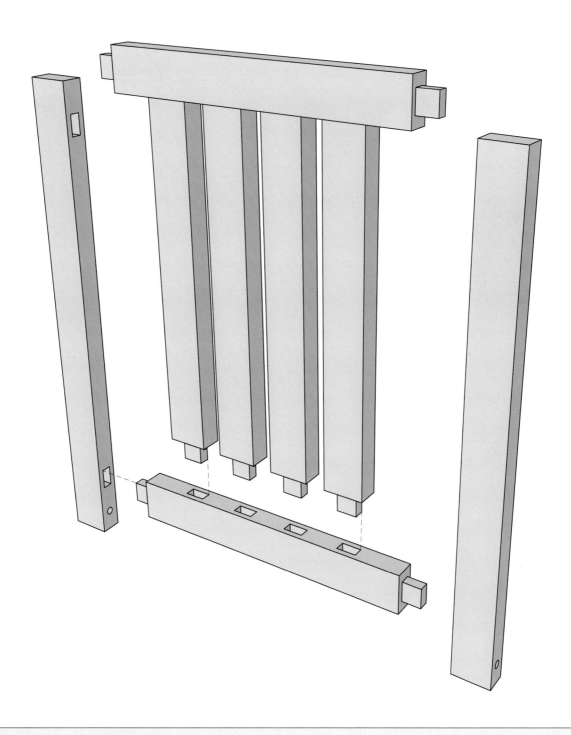

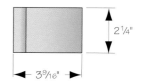

2¼"

3⁹⁄₁₆"

Each square represents 1".

5 Cut the rocker blanks to size and glue 3 boards face to face to create the rocker blanks. Make two of these assemblies. After the glue dries, draw the outline of the rocker on the blank and cut it out using a band saw or jigsaw. Shape it using a hand plane, spoke shave, a disc and/or spindle sander.

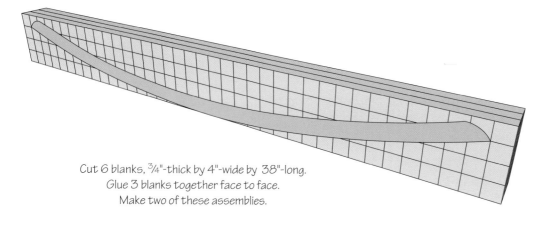

Cut 6 blanks, ¾"-thick by 4"-wide by 38"-long.
Glue 3 blanks together face to face.
Make two of these assemblies.

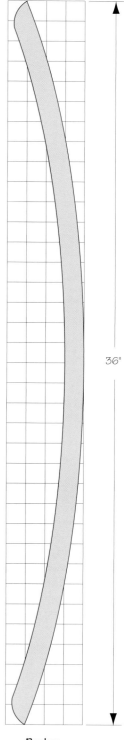

36"

Rocker

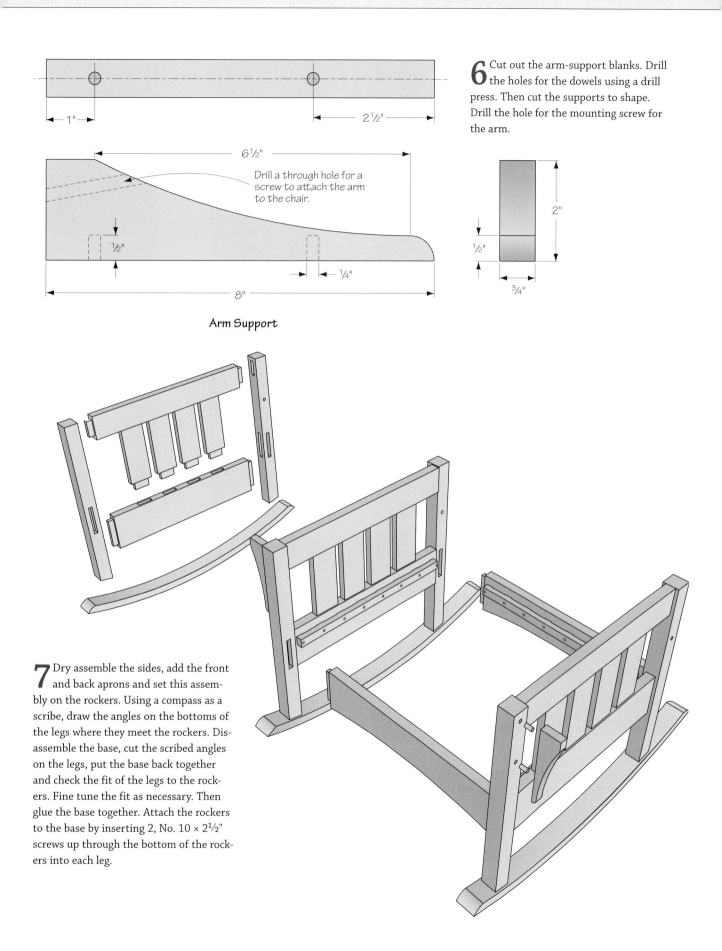

6 Cut out the arm-support blanks. Drill the holes for the dowels using a drill press. Then cut the supports to shape. Drill the hole for the mounting screw for the arm.

1"

2½"

6½"

Drill a through hole for a screw to attach the arm to the chair.

½"

¼"

8"

2"

½"

¾"

Arm Support

7 Dry assemble the sides, add the front and back aprons and set this assembly on the rockers. Using a compass as a scribe, draw the angles on the bottoms of the legs where they meet the rockers. Disassemble the base, cut the scribed angles on the legs, put the base back together and check the fit of the legs to the rockers. Fine tune the fit as necessary. Then glue the base together. Attach the rockers to the base by inserting 2, No. 10 × 2½" screws up through the bottom of the rockers into each leg.

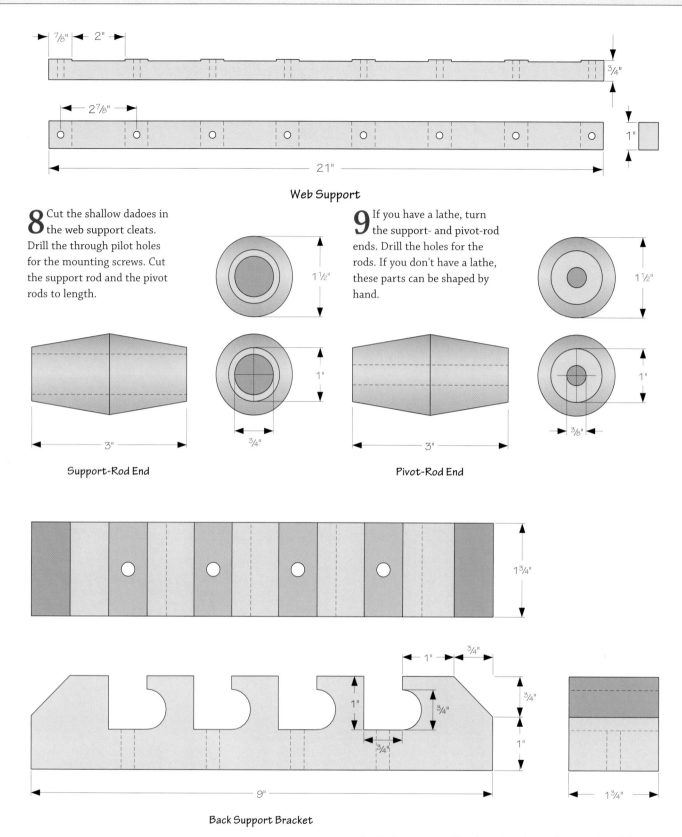

Web Support

8 Cut the shallow dadoes in the web support cleats. Drill the through pilot holes for the mounting screws. Cut the support rod and the pivot rods to length.

9 If you have a lathe, turn the support- and pivot-rod ends. Drill the holes for the rods. If you don't have a lathe, these parts can be shaped by hand.

Support-Rod End

Pivot-Rod End

Back Support Bracket

10 Cut a piece of hardwood to the thickness and width of the support brackets, and leave it about 20" long. Lay out the notches for each bracket. Use a drill press and a ¾" Forstner bit to cut the round parts of the notches. Use a table saw to cut the notches to size. Cut the brackets to length and cut the miters on the ends. Then drill the mounting-screw holes.

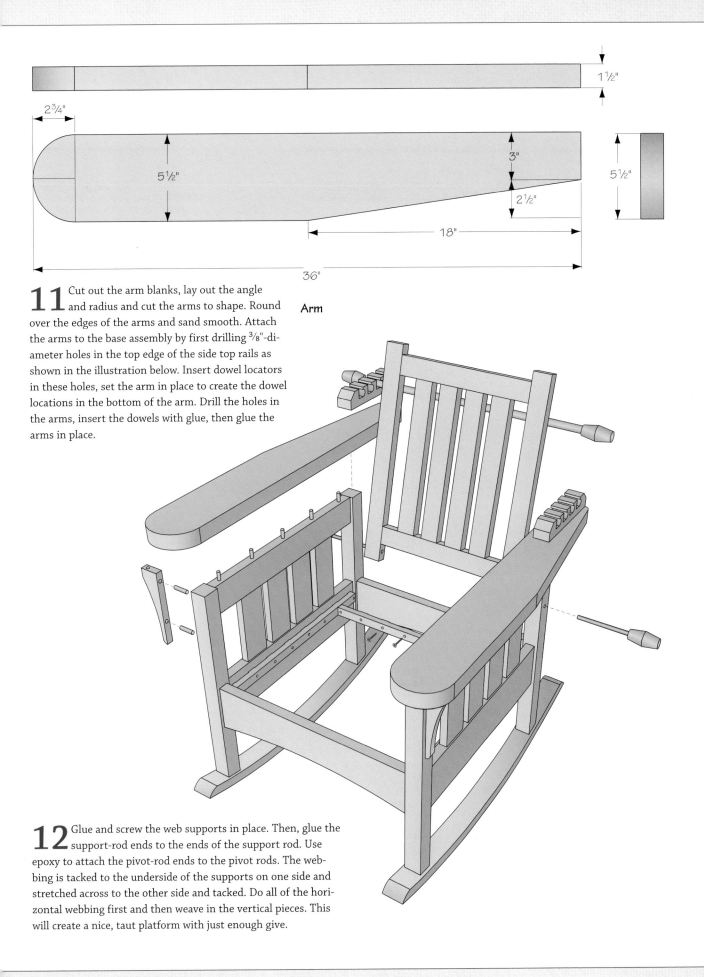

Arm

11 Cut out the arm blanks, lay out the angle and radius and cut the arms to shape. Round over the edges of the arms and sand smooth. Attach the arms to the base assembly by first drilling ³⁄₈"-diameter holes in the top edge of the side top rails as shown in the illustration below. Insert dowel locators in these holes, set the arm in place to create the dowel locations in the bottom of the arm. Drill the holes in the arms, insert the dowels with glue, then glue the arms in place.

12 Glue and screw the web supports in place. Then, glue the support-rod ends to the ends of the support rod. Use epoxy to attach the pivot-rod ends to the pivot rods. The webbing is tacked to the underside of the supports on one side and stretched across to the other side and tacked. Do all of the horizontal webbing first and then weave in the vertical pieces. This will create a nice, taut platform with just enough give.

GLASS-TOP LAMP TABLE

Both Craftsman- and Mission-style furniture enjoyed a great deal of popularity during the late 19th and 20th centuries. The glass-top lamp table presented here incorporates elements derived from both styles. The soft sweep of the lower aprons can be attributed to the Mission influence (the Harvey Ellis curves), while the vertical stringers owe their origin to the Craftsman style.

Made of cherry and given a cherry stain, this table will be at home in a den or front room. The top features a quarter-inch thick piece of bronzed tempered glass.

inches (millimeters)

REFERENCE	QUANTITY	PART	STOCK	THICKNESS	(mm)	WIDTH	(mm)	LENGTH	(mm)	COMMENTS
A	4	legs	hardwood	1¾	(44)	1¾	(44)	24	(610)	
B	2	front/back top aprons	hardwood	1¹⁄₁₆	(27)	3	(76)	20	(508)	
C	2	side top aprons	hardwood	1¹⁄₁₆	(27)	3	(76)	20	(508)	
D	4	top rails	hardwood	1¹⁄₁₆	(27)	5	(127)	28	(711)	
E	2	bottom side aprons	hardwood	1¹⁄₁₆	(27)	5	(127)	20	(508)	
F	2	front/back bottom aprons	hardwood	1¹⁄₁₆	(27)	4	(102)	20	(508)	
G	1	bottom shelf	hardwood	¾	(19)	22¹⁄₁₆	(560)	19½	(495)	cut to fit
H	4	top supports	hardwood	¾	(19)	2½	(63.5)	8	(203)	
I	10	stringers	hardwood	¾	(19)	2	(51)	11½	(292)	
J	2	side cleats	hardwood	¾	(19)	⅝	(16)	18½	(470)	
K	2	front/back cleats	hardwood	¾	(19)	⅝	(16)	17⅞	(454)	
	1	tinted or clear, tempered glass	tempered	¼	(6)	19½	(495)	19½	(495)	buy glass before building project

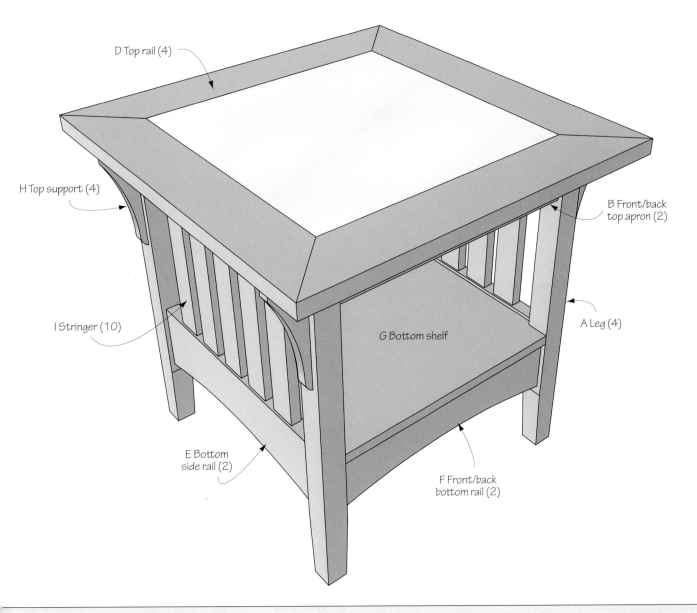

D Top rail (4)

H Top support (4)

B Front/back top apron (2)

I Stringer (10)

G Bottom shelf

A Leg (4)

E Bottom side rail (2)

F Front/back bottom rail (2)

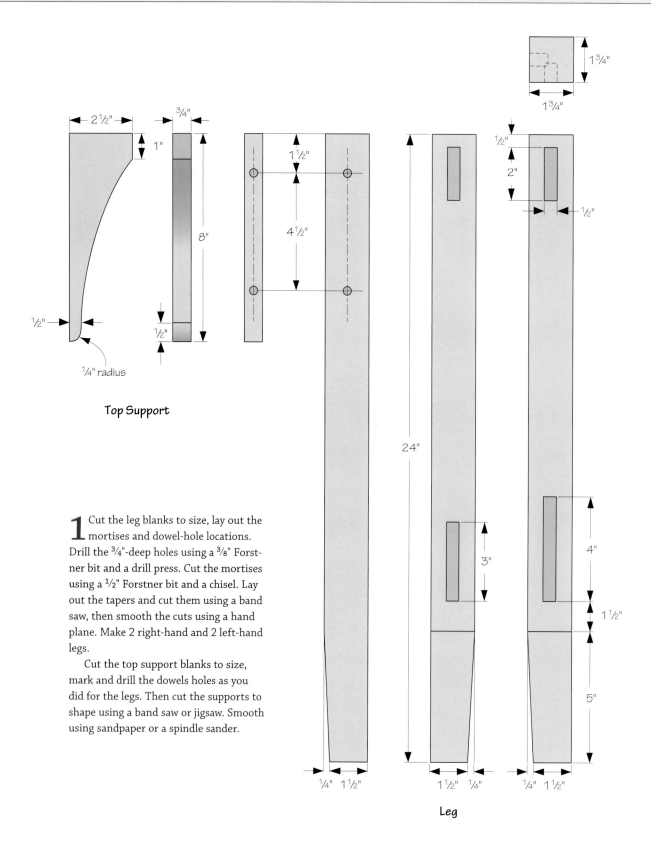

Top Support

1 Cut the leg blanks to size, lay out the mortises and dowel-hole locations. Drill the ¾"-deep holes using a ⅜" Forstner bit and a drill press. Cut the mortises using a ½" Forstner bit and a chisel. Lay out the tapers and cut them using a band saw, then smooth the cuts using a hand plane. Make 2 right-hand and 2 left-hand legs.

Cut the top support blanks to size, mark and drill the dowels holes as you did for the legs. Then cut the supports to shape using a band saw or jigsaw. Smooth using sandpaper or a spindle sander.

Leg

2 Cut and fit the tenons, on the aprons, to the mortises in the legs. Cut the grooves on the table saw, then, cut the curve on the bottom apron using a band saw. Smooth the curve using a spindle sander.

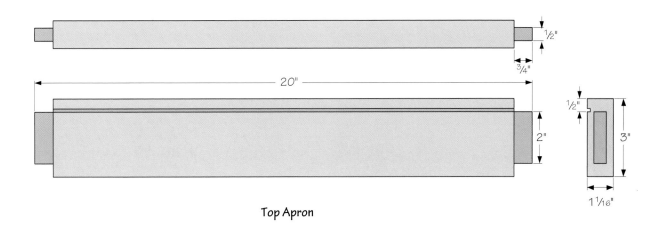

Top Apron

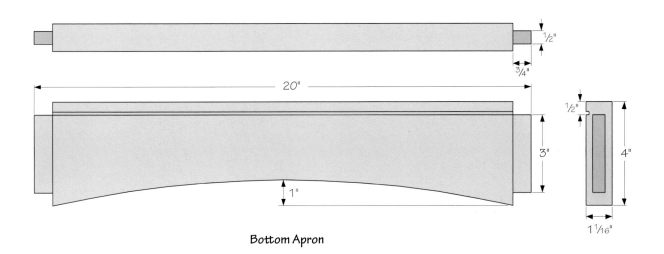

Bottom Apron

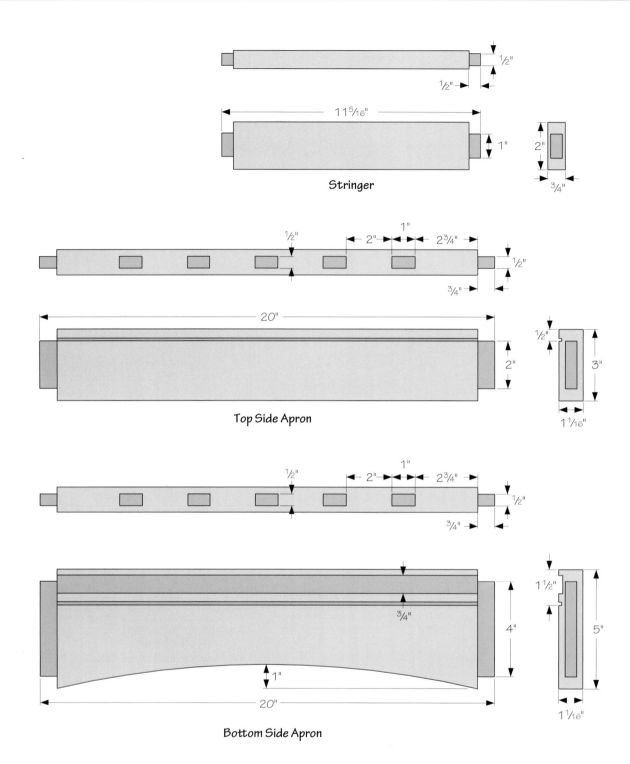

Stringer

Top Side Apron

Bottom Side Apron

3 Cut and fit the tenons on the top and bottom side aprons to fit the mortises in the legs. Then cut the mortises in the aprons. Cut the tenons on the stringers to fit the tenons in the aprons. Cut the curve in the bottom side aprons.

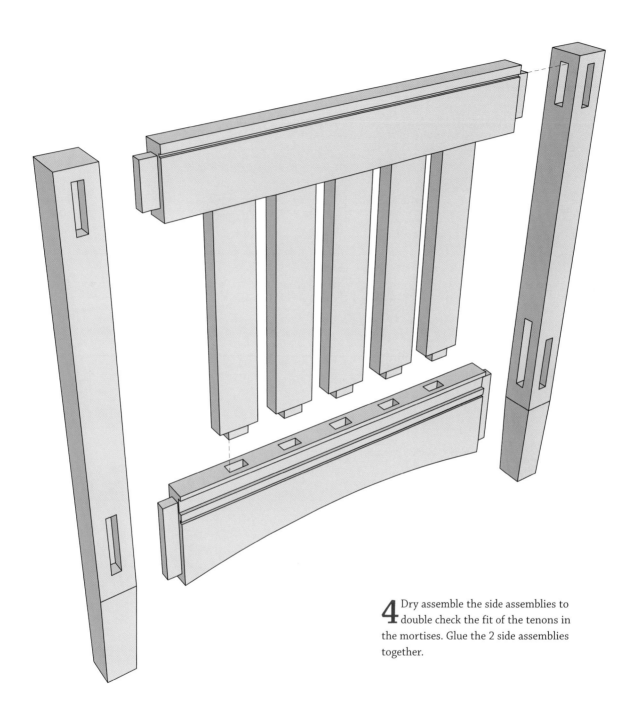

4 Dry assemble the side assemblies to double check the fit of the tenons in the mortises. Glue the 2 side assemblies together.

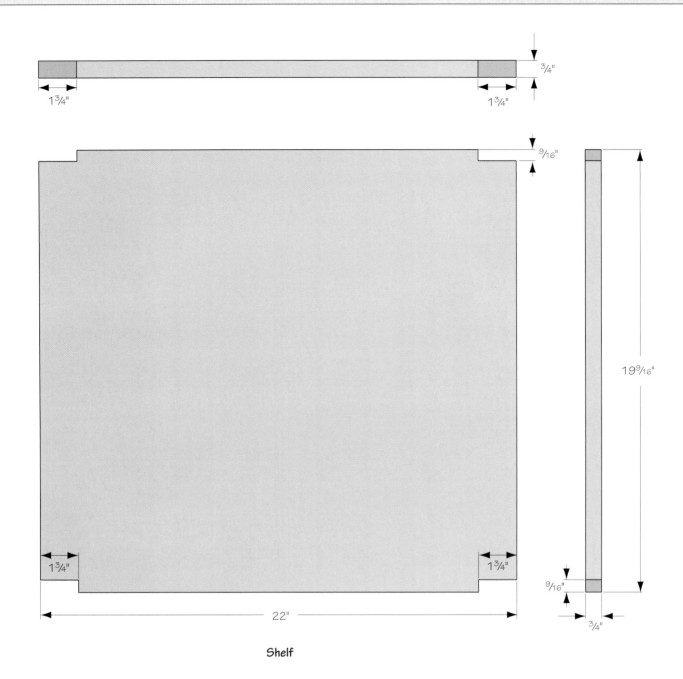

3/4"

1 3/4"

1 3/4"

9/16"

19 9/16"

1 3/4"

1 3/4"

9/16"

3/4"

22"

Shelf

5 Dry assemble the side assemblies to each other with the remaining aprons. Double check the fit of the shelf, Then cut the shelf to size and cut the notches using a table saw, band saw or hand saw.

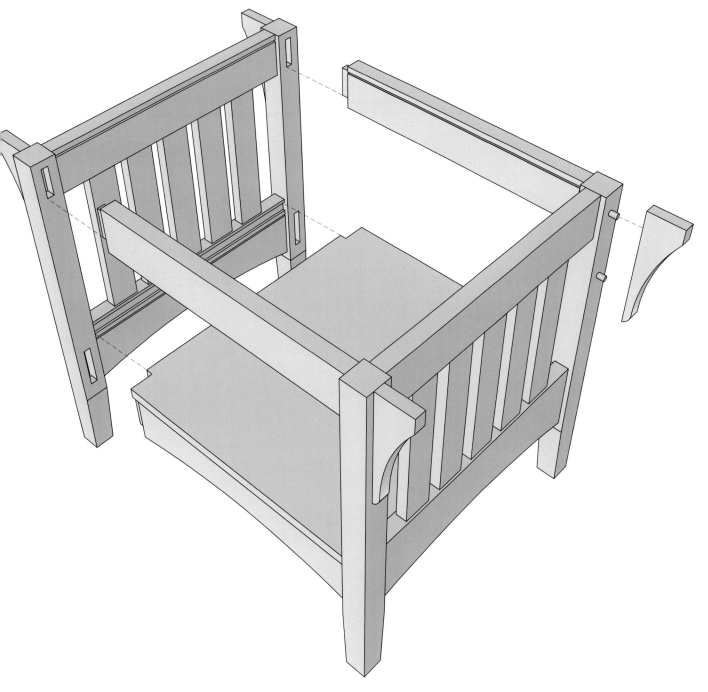

6 Glue the side assemblies, shelf and aprons together. Attach the shelf in place using 8 tabletop fasteners. Glue the top supports in place using dowels.

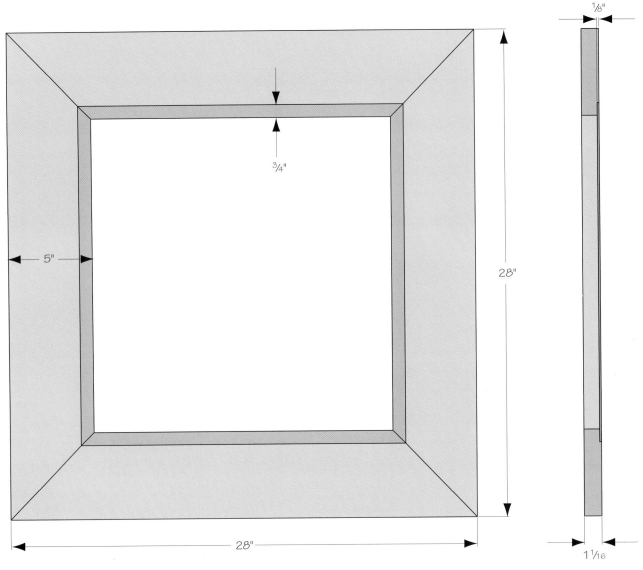

Top Frame

7 Before making the top frame, purchase a piece of tempered glass to the size shown in the cutting list. Then cut the top frame parts to size and rough length and cut the rabbet to the size needed, approximately ¼"-deep by ½"-wide, for the glass top. Cut the miters using a miter gauge on your table saw, a power miter saw or a miter box and a hand saw. When cutting these miters, carefully measure your glass top to ensure you cut the frame parts to the correct length.

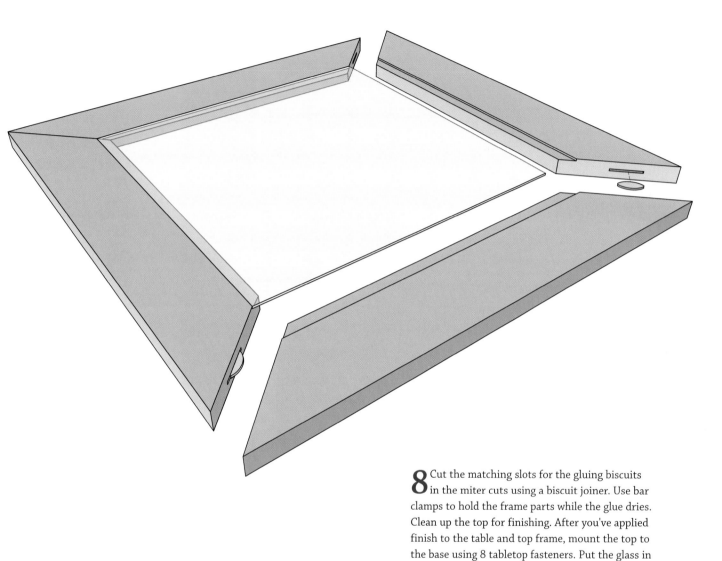

8 Cut the matching slots for the gluing biscuits in the miter cuts using a biscuit joiner. Use bar clamps to hold the frame parts while the glue dries. Clean up the top for finishing. After you've applied finish to the table and top frame, mount the top to the base using 8 tabletop fasteners. Put the glass in place and enjoy.

MISSION-STYLE DRESSING-TABLE MIRROR

This mirror closely follows the Mission design, which is simple but elegant, and will complement most any decor. The preferred location for the mirror is to hang it above a dresser in the bedroom. It's made of cherry and has a cherry stain, to enhance the natural cherry color.

inches (millimeters)

REFERENCE	QUANTITY	PART	STOCK	THICKNESS	(mm)	WIDTH	(mm)	LENGTH	(mm)	COMMENTS
A	2	stiles	hardwood	1$^{1}/_{16}$	(27)	2$^{1}/_{2}$	(64)	36	(914)	
B	1	bottom rail	hardwood	1$^{1}/_{16}$	(27)	3$^{1}/_{2}$	(89)	20$^{1}/_{2}$	(521)	
C	1	top rail	hardwood	1$^{1}/_{16}$	(27)	7	(178)	20$^{1}/_{2}$	(521)	
	1	back	hardboard	$^{1}/_{4}$	(6)	19$^{11}/_{16}$	(500)	29$^{1}/_{8}$	(740)	measure after frame is assembled
	1	foam board		$^{1}/_{8}$	(3)	19$^{11}/_{16}$	(500)	28$^{1}/_{2}$	(724)	measure after frame is assembled
	1	mirror	glass	$^{1}/_{8}$	(3)					

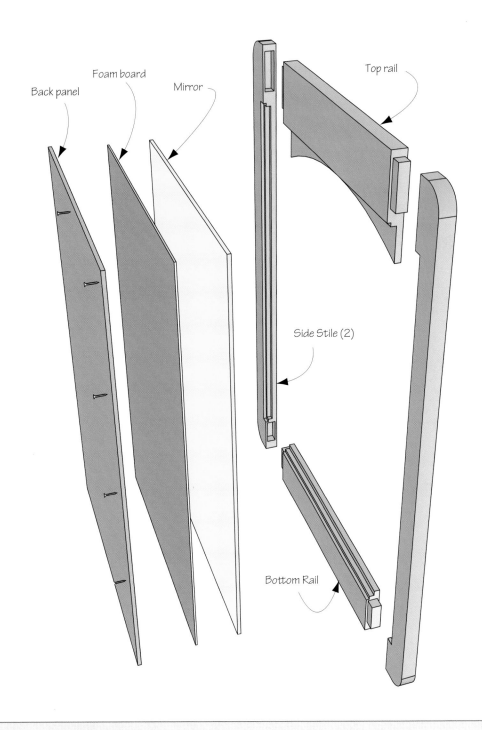

Back panel

Foam board

Mirror

Top rail

Side Stile (2)

Bottom Rail

1 Cut the stile and rail blanks to size. Three operations need to be performed on the 2 stiles: Routing stopped rabbets, mortising the ends to receive the rail tenons and rounding the ends of the stiles.

Lay out the dimensions of the rabbets. A router or a router mounted in a router table can be used to cut these and is done in two steps. First, cut the ¼"-deep rabbets, then cut the ⅝"-deep rabbets. In order to maintain the same dimension on the rabbets, rout both stiles before changing the depth of the router bit for the second set of rabbets. The bottom and top rails should be routed at the same time as the 2 stiles. Square the ends of the stopped rabbets with a chisel.

Cut the mortises in the stiles and cut the tenons on the rails to fit these mortises. Finally, make the radius cuts on the stiles and the arch on the bottom rail using a band saw or jig saw.

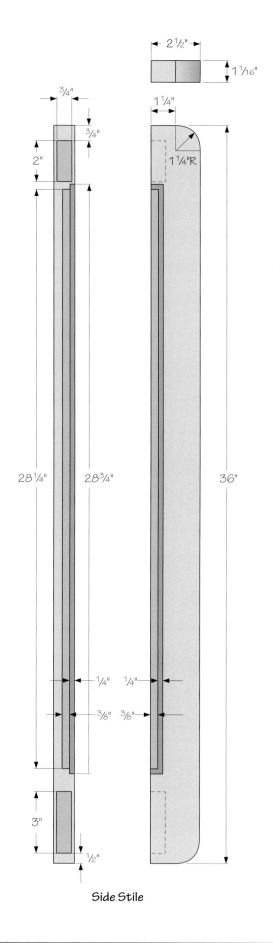

Side Stile

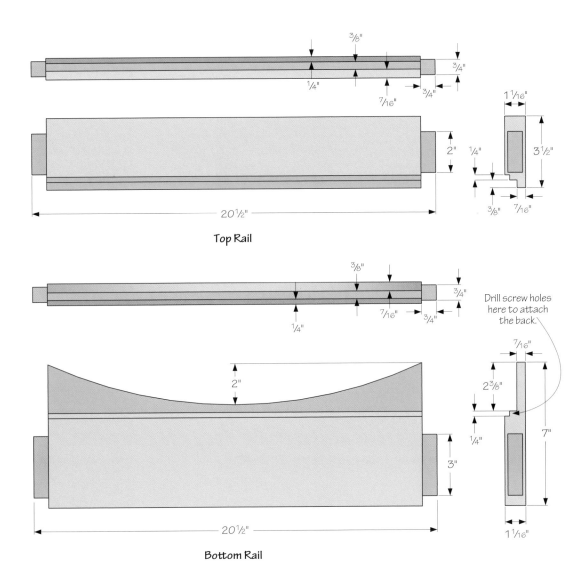

Top Rail

Bottom Rail

Drill screw holes here to attach the back.

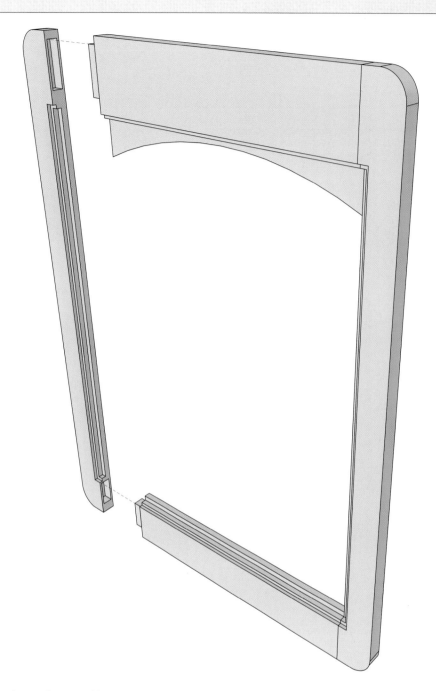

2 As always, dry assemble the mirror frame to double check that all the parts fit together properly, then glue the frame together. Measure the exact cutting sizes of the foam board and the back. The mirror's measurements should be $\frac{1}{8}$" less in the width and length than the true dimensions and $\frac{1}{4}$" thick. This $\frac{1}{8}$" gives you some room for slight errors when the mirror is cut. Or, if you prefer, you can purchase the mirror first and make the frame to fit it.

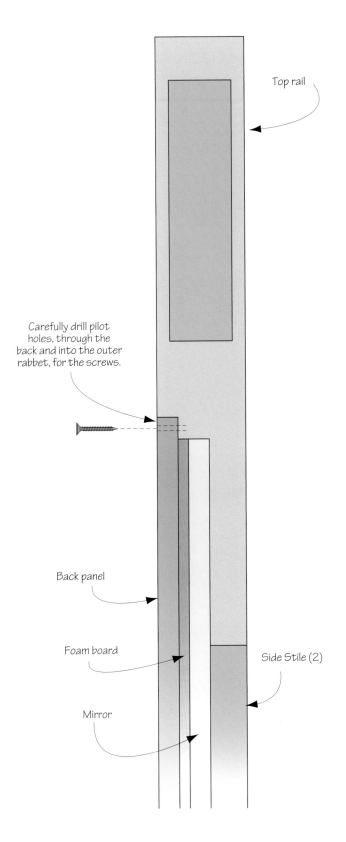

Top rail

Carefully drill pilot holes, through the back and into the outer rabbet, for the screws.

Back panel

Foam board

Mirror

Side Stile (2)

3 Attach the back by drilling pilot holes through the back and into the shallowest rabbet of the frame. Be careful when drilling these holes to ensure against drilling into the rabbet that holds the mirror and foam board.

DROP-LEAF TABLE

This table will be at home as a side table or as an occasional table. Made from cherry, it was finished with a few coats of polyurethane. Tung oil varnish can also be used.

inches (millimeters)

REFERENCE	QUANTITY	PART	STOCK	THICKNESS	(mm)	WIDTH	(mm)	LENGTH	(mm)	COMMENTS
A	1	top center	hardwood	$^3\!/_4$	(19)	10	(254)	24	(610)	
B	2	top side leaves	hardwood	$^3\!/_4$	(19)	9	(229)	24	(610)	
C	2	top cleats	hardwood	$1^1\!/_{16}$	(27)	2	(51)	8	(203)	
D	2	side center top	hardwood	$^3\!/_4$	(19)	2	(51)	$3^3\!/_4$	(95)	
E	2	side center bottom	hardwood	$^3\!/_4$	(19)	2	(51)	$5^3\!/_4$	(146)	
F	4	side outside verticals	hardwood	$^3\!/_4$	(19)	$1^1\!/_2$	(38)	$19^1\!/_2$	(495)	
G	2	feet	hardwood	$1^1\!/_{16}$	(27)	3	(76)	$13^1\!/_2$	(343)	
H	1	shelf	hardwood	$^3\!/_4$	(19)	5	(127)	$17^5\!/_8$	(448)	
I	2	swivel bases	hardwood	$^3\!/_4$	(19)	$^3\!/_4$	(19)	3	(76)	
J	2	swivels	hardwood	$^3\!/_4$	(19)	$1^1\!/_2$	(38)	10	(254)	
	4	dowels	hardwood	$^3\!/_8$	(9.5)	$^3\!/_4$	(19)			
	2	drop-leaf hinge/pair	hardwood							Woodcraft #16R41 or equivalent

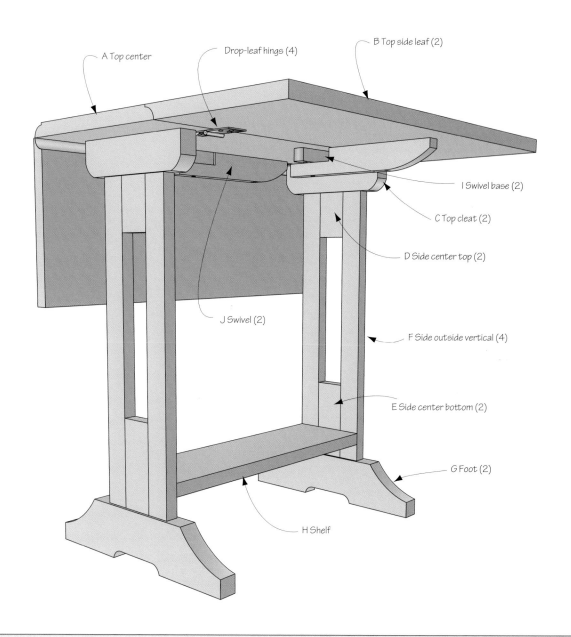

A Top center

Drop-leaf hings (4)

B Top side leaf (2)

I Swivel base (2)

C Top cleat (2)

D Side center top (2)

J Swivel (2)

F Side outside vertical (4)

E Side center bottom (2)

G Foot (2)

H Shelf

1 Cut the top cleat blanks to size. Lay out for the dowel holes, and, using a drill press with a ⅜" Forstner bit, bore the holes ⅜" deep. Make the radius cuts using a band saw or jigsaw.

Cut the foot blanks to size, lay out the mortise and cut it using a ½" Forstner bit and a chisel. Then cut the top curves and the lower cut out.

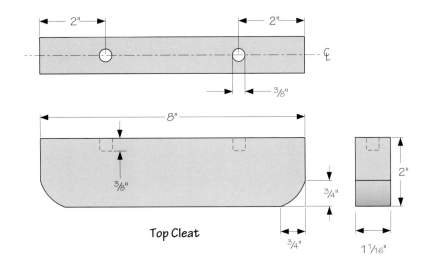

Top Cleat

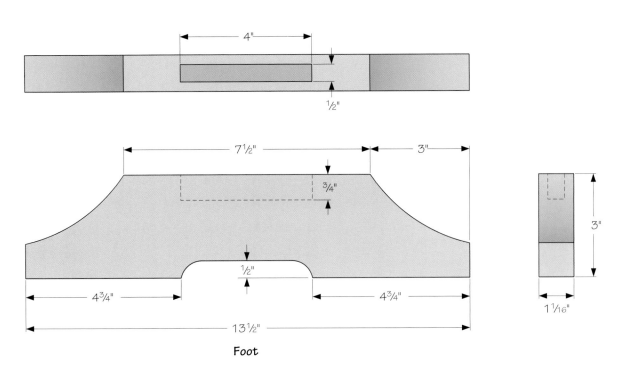

Foot

2 The top and bottom spacers and the side outside verticals are glued together before cutting the tenons or dadoes. First, cut out the top spacers, bottom spacers and the side outside verticals to size. Then glue them together as shown in the illustration on the next page.

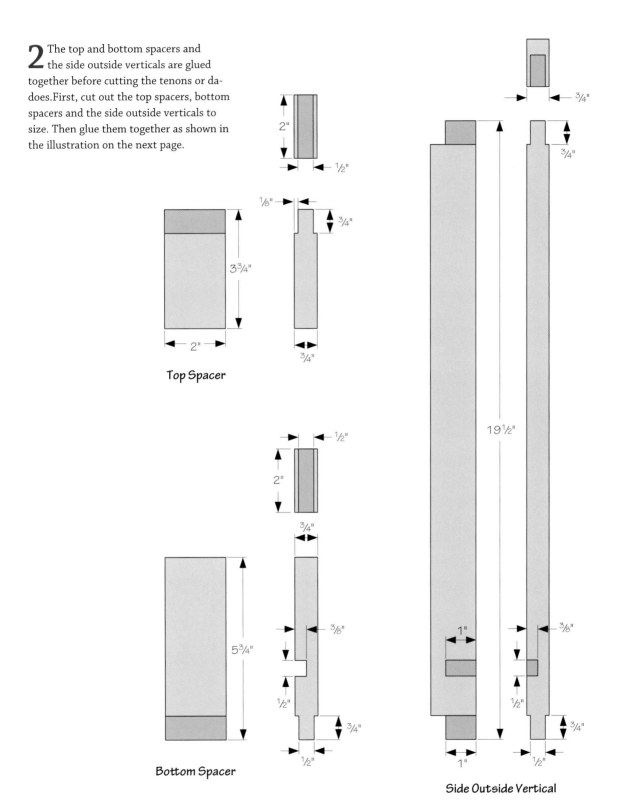

Top Spacer

Bottom Spacer

Side Outside Vertical

3 This illustrations shows the side parts as they relate to each other. As stated in Step 2, the top and bottom spacers and the side outside verticals are glued together before cutting the tenons or dadoes.

The tenons are cut to fit the mortises in the feet and the top cleats. Then cut the dadoes using a router and a straightedge to guide the router. Square the stopped ends of the dadoes using a chisel.

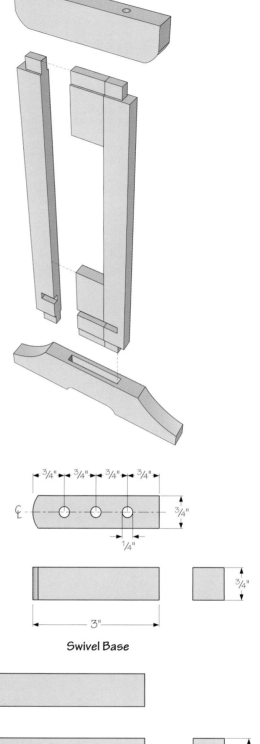

4 Cut the swivel and swivel base parts to size. Use a drill press to bore the ¼"-diameter through holes. Cut the notch in the swivel using a table saw with a miter gauge, set to cut squarely, with a sacrificial face attached to it, or, use a band saw. Finally, round the ends of the swivel bases using some sandpaper or a disc sander.

Swivel Base

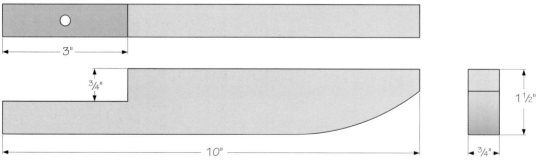

Swivel

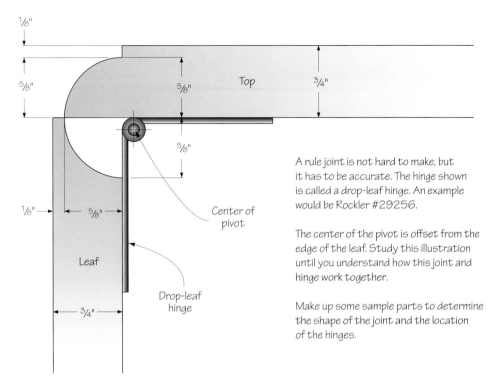

5 The rule joints on the top center and the top side leaves are easy to cut using a matched set of router bits. Cut some extra scrap parts to practice cutting the rule joint. When you've got your setups tuned in, cut the joints. The best tool for making these cuts is a router table. It's safe and very accurate. See the illustrations on the following pages showing how the setups look.

Before installing the hinges on the top parts, practice on some scraps that have the matching rule-joint cuts. Start by turning the parts upside down, pull the rule joint tight and install the hinges. Double check to ensure the top and the leaf don't rub on each other at the joint. When you're good to go, install the hinges 4" from each end of the top.

A rule joint is not hard to make, but it has to be accurate. The hinge shown is called a drop-leaf hinge. An example would be Rockler #29256.

The center of the pivot is offset from the edge of the leaf. Study this illustration until you understand how this joint and hinge work together.

Make up some sample parts to determine the shape of the joint and the location of the hinges.

Full-Scale Rule (or Drop-Leaf) Joint Layout

6 When setting up the router table, exact measurements will get you in the ballpark, but the final tuning of the cut is trial and error. Use wood scraps that are the same thickness as the tabletop parts. Once you get your cut where you like it, make the cuts in the top. Make a cut on each long edge of the center top part.

Remember, the top will have the stepped roundover cut.

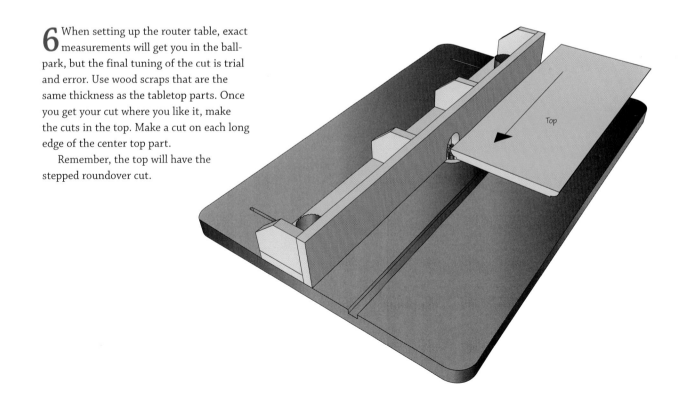

7 Match the stepped cove cut to the roundover cut on the center top. Again, this may take a few trial-and-error cuts to get it right. Be sure to use scrap wood to fine tune the cut before making the cut on the leaves. Rout one long edge only or each leaf.

Remember, the leaves will have the stepped cove cut.

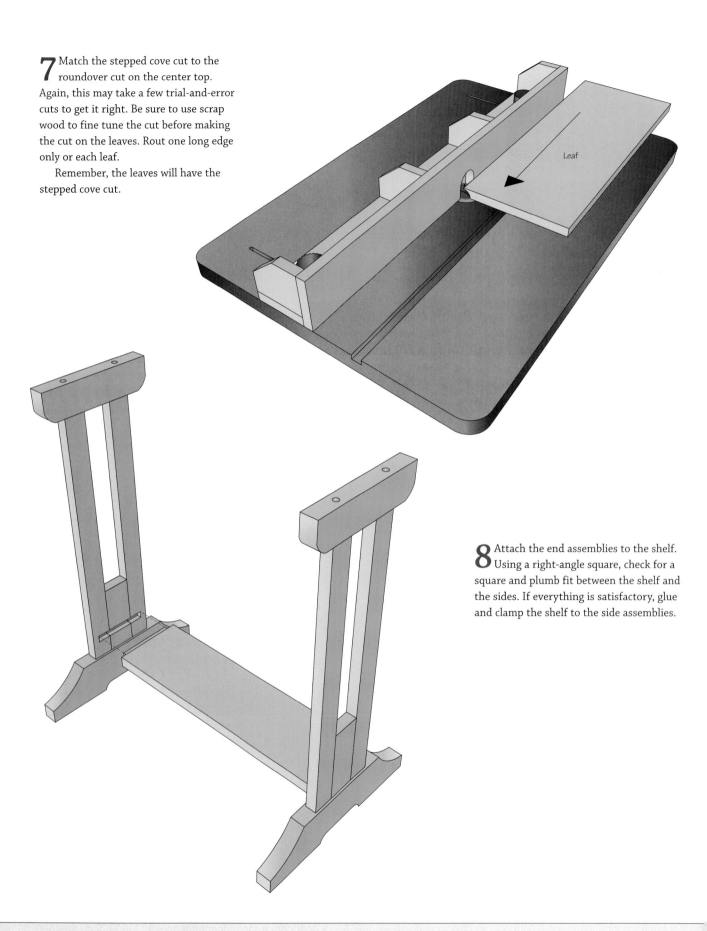

Leaf

8 Attach the end assemblies to the shelf. Using a right-angle square, check for a square and plumb fit between the shelf and the sides. If everything is satisfactory, glue and clamp the shelf to the side assemblies.

9 Invert the top on your bench and center the base assemble on the top. Mark the locations of the top cleats. Now, turn the base over and insert dowel centers into the holes in the top cleats. Turn the base over and locate it on the top using the marks you drew. Using the marks made by the dowel inserts, drill the ³⁄₈"-diameter holes ³⁄₈" deep. Add glue to the dowels and insert them into the holes. Fit the base in place and clamp it until the glue dries.

10 Lay out the locations for the swivel bases and glue and screw them in place. Attach the swivel arms, tightening the screws just enough so the arms rotate snugly. Refer to the installation instructions that came with the hinges and attach the hinges to the center top and the drop leaves. Locate the hinges 4" from each end of the top.

PLANT STAND

This Arts & Crafts plant holder is easy to build, and emulates the design of furniture of this era. This stand will hold medium and small plants and will compliment the decor of many settings. The stand is built from cherry and stained with a cherry gel stain. A tung-oil varnish was applied. If you so desire, the project could remain unstained and let time darken the finish.

inches (millimeters)

REFERENCE	QUANTITY	PART	STOCK	THICKNESS	(mm)	WIDTH	(mm)	LENGTH	(mm)	COMMENTS
A	4	legs	hardwood	1³⁄₄	(44)	1³⁄₄	(44)	30	(762)	
B	2	upper side aprons	hardwood	1¹⁄₁₆	(27)	3	(76)	9¹⁄₄	(235)	
C	2	lower side aprons	hardwood	1¹⁄₁₆	(27)	4	(102)	9¹⁄₄	(235)	
D	2	upper front/back aprons	hardwood	1¹⁄₁₆	(27)	3	(76)	18¹⁄₄	(464)	
E	2	lower front/back aprons	hardwood	1¹⁄₁₆	(27)	4	(102)	18¹⁄₄	(464)	
F	2	shelves	hardwood	³⁄₄	(19)	9	(229)	18	(457)	cut to fit

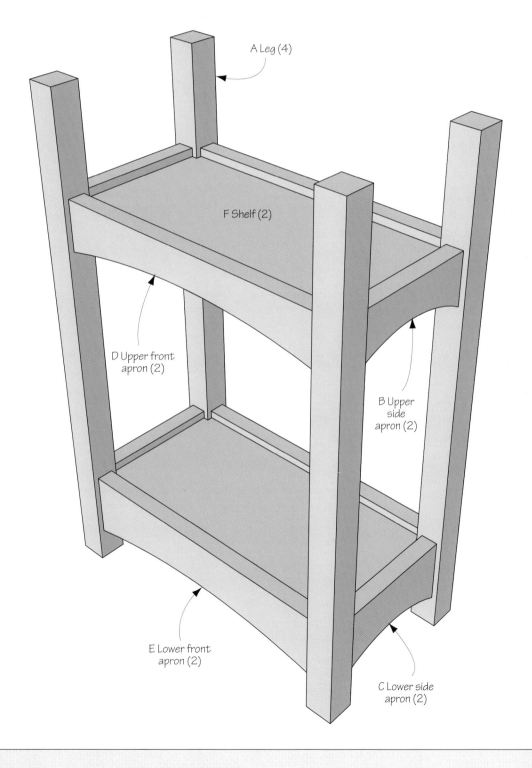

A Leg (4)

F Shelf (2)

D Upper front apron (2)

B Upper side apron (2)

E Lower front apron (2)

C Lower side apron (2)

1 Cut the leg blanks to size, lay out the mortises and cut them using a ¹⁄₂" Forstner bit and a chisel.

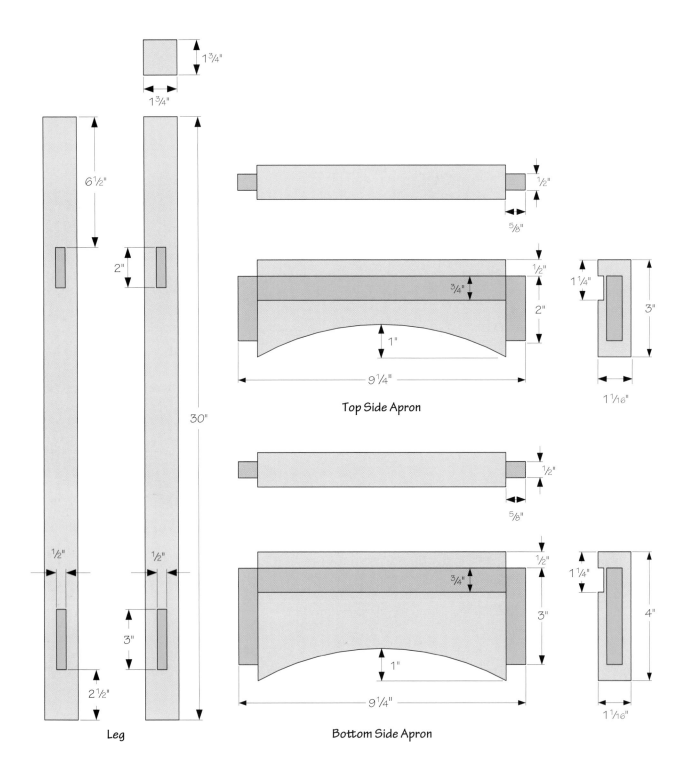

Leg

Top Side Apron

Bottom Side Apron

2 Cut out the top and bottom side aprons and the top front and bottom apron blanks to size. Cut the tenons to fit the mortises in the legs. Then cut the grooves for the shelf using the table saw. Finally, lay out the curves and cut them using a band saw or jigsaw.

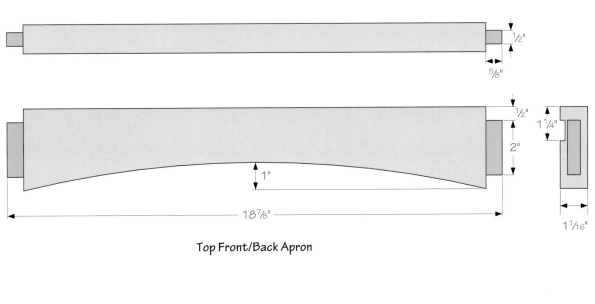

½"

5⁄8"

½"

1¼"

2"

1"

18⅞"

1 1⁄16"

Top Front/Back Apron

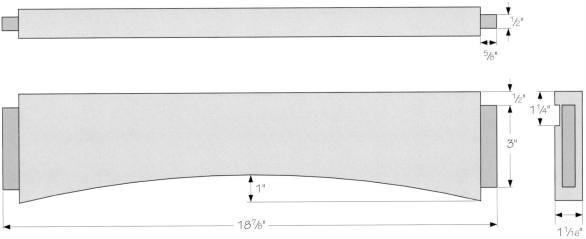

½"

5⁄8"

½"

1¼"

3"

1"

18⅞"

1 1⁄16"

Bottom Front/Back Apron

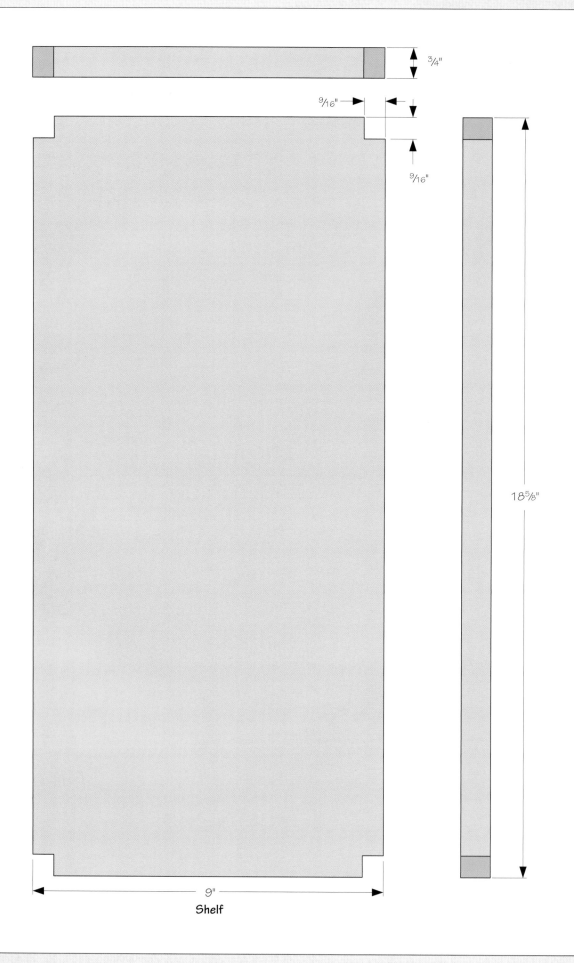

3/4"

9/16"

9/16"

18⅝"

9"

Shelf

3 Dry assemble the base. Double check the measurements for the shelves, then cut the shelves to size. Cut the notches using a band saw. Glue the side sub assemblies together. After the glue dries, fit the shelves between the top front/back and bottom front/back aprons, then glue the side assemblies to the aprons. Don't apply glue to the shelves. Let them float because the dadoes will hold them in place.

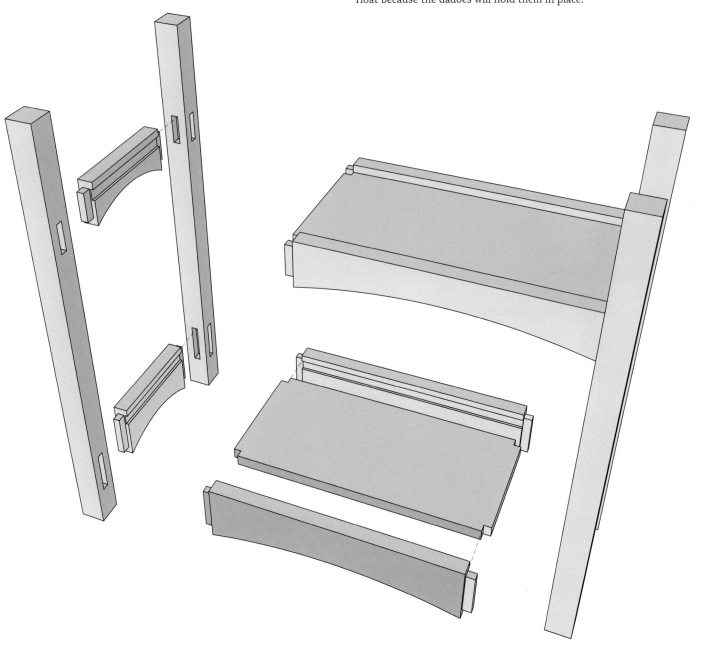

WALL-MOUNTED CLOCK

This little clock is simple to build and emulated a Mission styled, or Arts & Crafts era piece of furniture and should make a great weekend project. Instead of being mounted in a frame that is sort of square, I made the frame rectangular with graceful curves and is still in keeping with that era. The clock works include a pendulum and a Westminster chime. All parts are make from cherry wood. Finishing is very simple. The completed project was given a slight cherry stain and finally finished with three coats of tung oil.

inches (millimeters)

REFERENCE	QUANTITY	PART	STOCK	THICKNESS	(mm)	WIDTH	(mm)	LENGTH	(mm)	COMMENTS
A	1	back	hardwood	¾	(19)	9	(229)	18	(457)	
B	2	supports	hardwood	¾	(19)	2	(51)	6	(152)	
C	1	box top	hardwood	¾	(19)	2½	(63.5)	7	(178)	
D	2	box sides	hardwood	¾	(19)	2½	(63.5)	8	(203)	
E	1	box bottom	hardwood	¾	(19)	¾	(19)	7	(178)	
F	1	box front	hardwood	¼	(6)	8	(203)	8	(203)	
G	4	box front trim	hardwood	⅝	(16)	⅝	(16)	10	(254)	cut parts to fit

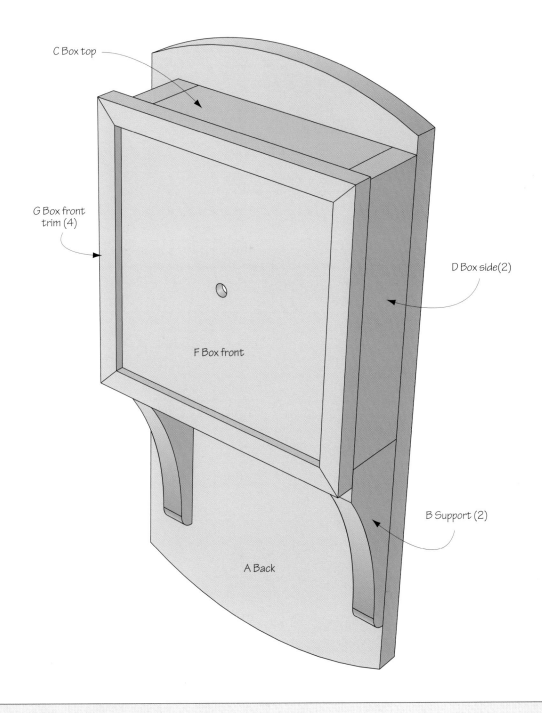

C Box top

G Box front trim (4)

D Box side (2)

F Box front

B Support (2)

A Back

1 Cut out the back as per the illustration. Drill ½" starter holes at each corner of the hole, then cut the hole using a jigsaw. Round over the ends using a band saw or jigsaw. Smooth the curves using a disc sander or sandpaper wrapped around a block.

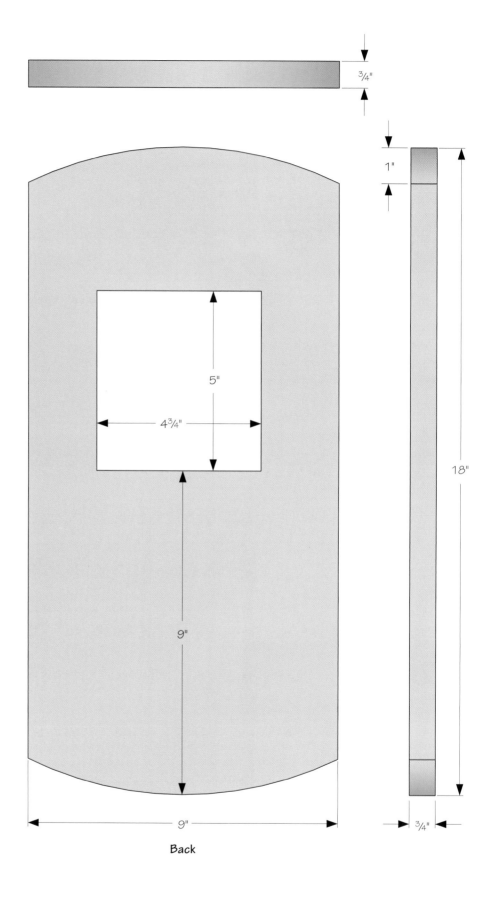

Back

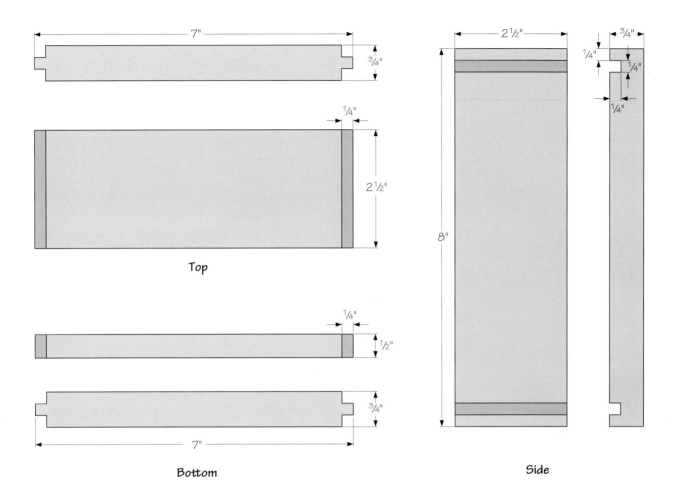

Top

Bottom

Side

2 Cut the box parts to size. Use a table saw to cut the dadoes in the sides. Cut the on the top and bottom parts to fit the dadoes in the sides.

3 Glue the box together as shown in the illustration.

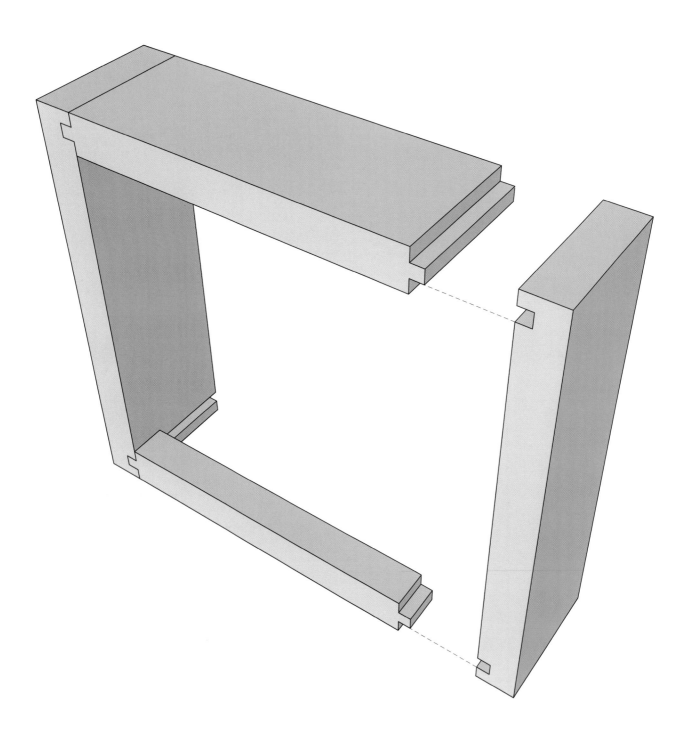

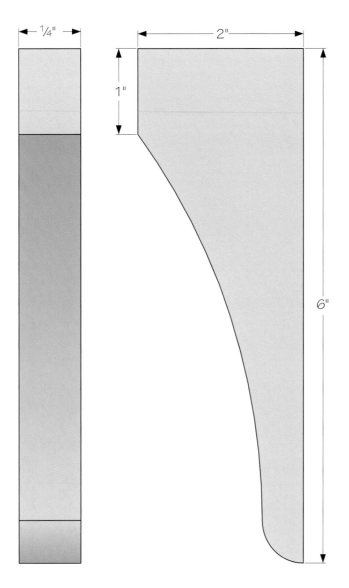

Support

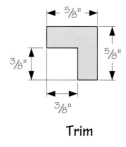

Trim

4 Cut the support blanks to size, lay out the curves and cut them using a band saw or jigsaw. Smooth the curves with a spindle sander.

Dimension the trim blanks to thickness. Make a couple of blanks to thickness and about 2" wide and about 10" long. Leave each blank about 4 or 5" longer than the finished length. This extra width will make it safer and easier to cut a rabbet in each long edge of both blanks using a table saw. Then rip each trim piece to width from the blanks.

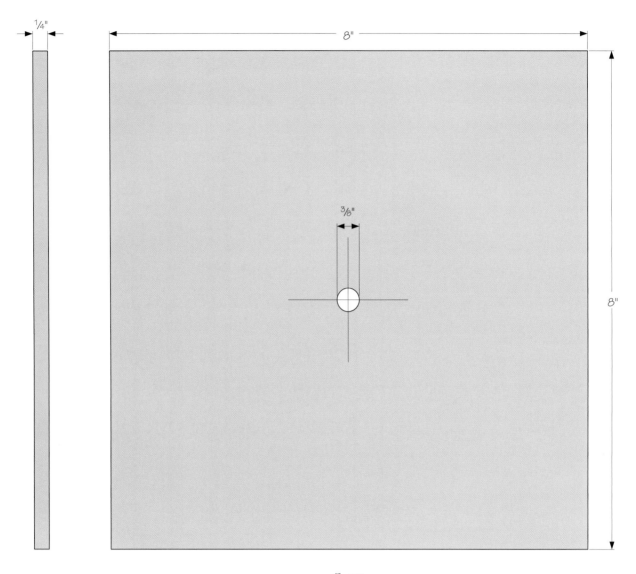

Front

5 Cut the clock front to size and drill a ³⁄₈"-diameter hole in the center.

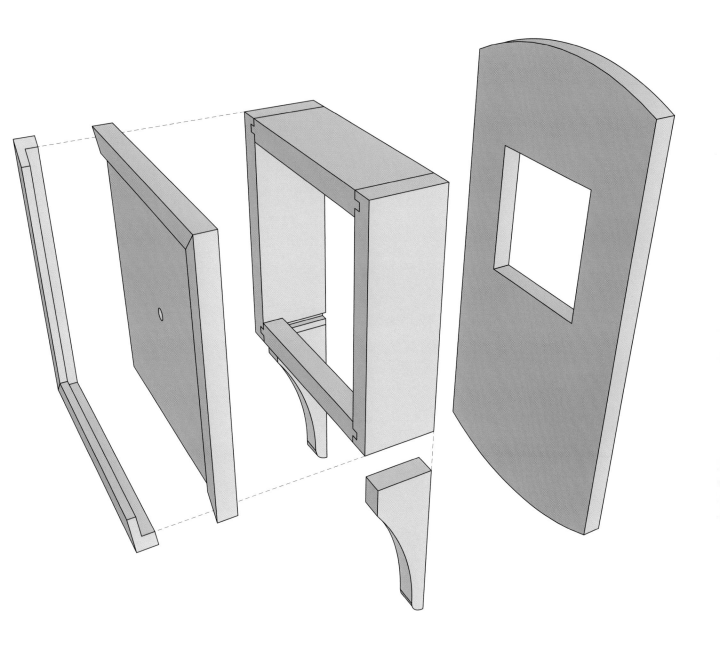

6 Screw the box to the back and glue the supports in place. Glue the face piece to the box. Attach the clock face to the face using some spray adhesive. Then cut the trim pieces to length and glue them in place.

Install the clock works as per the instructions that come with them.

GLASS SHELF ÉTAGÈRE

This project is fairly easy to build and could complement any room that contains Arts & Crafts or Mission furniture. The room, where two of these are displayed, has a fireplace. There is one etagère on each side of the fireplace. The display turned bowls and family pictures. One might consider this a weekend project. The only woodworking necessary is to fabricate four legs that will hold the three glass shelves.2

inches (millimeters)

REFERENCE	QUANTITY	PART	STOCK	THICKNESS	(mm)	WIDTH	(mm)	LENGTH	(mm)	COMMENTS
A	4	legs	hardwood	1¼	(32)	1⅞	(48)	37	(94)	
	3	tempered glass shelves		¼	(6)	13	(330)	22¼	(565)	
		RTA adhesive	clear silicone							

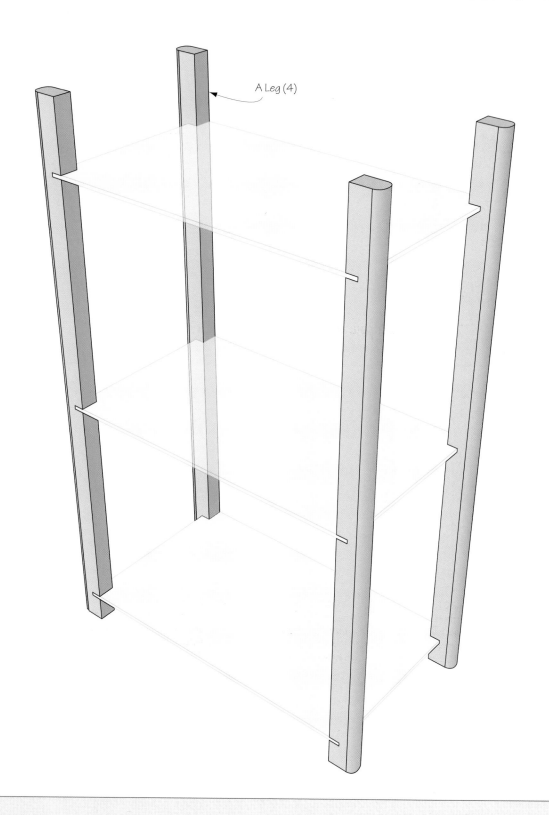

A Leg (4)

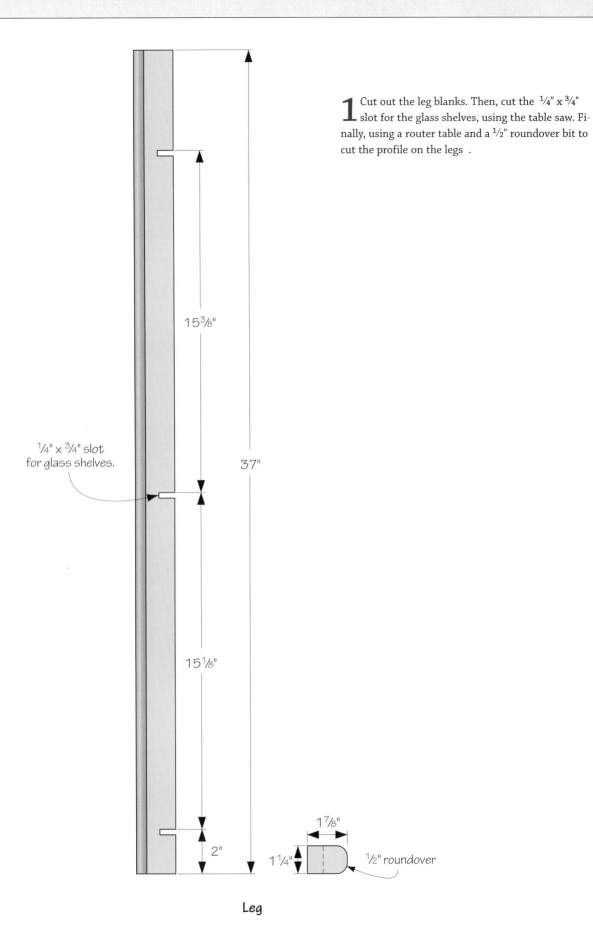

1 Cut out the leg blanks. Then, cut the ¼" x ¾" slot for the glass shelves, using the table saw. Finally, using a router table and a ½" roundover bit to cut the profile on the legs .

15³⁄₈"

¼" x ¾" slot for glass shelves.

37"

15¹⁄₈"

1⁷⁄₈"

2"

1¼"   ½" roundover

Leg

Tempered-Glass Shelf

22¼"

13"

¼"

GLASS-DOOR BOOKCASE

This bookcase has a history that goes back to the early 1900s and beyond. Initially it was seen as a square, boxy item. Then came along Gustav Stickley and a designer named Harvey Ellis, who worked for Stickley for a few months. Ellis is responsible for softening the Mission furniture designs and making them more pleasing to the eye.

For example, on a bookcase such as this, he added curved edges, such as the lower front apron. Ellis passed away while he was employed by Stickley, but in that time he revolutionized their furniture line. Since that time, curved surfaces on Mission furniture has been referred to as the Harvey Ellis curve.

This bookcase is made from solid cherry and most of a sheet of quarter-inch plywood. The project is left unstained and three coats of polyurethane have been applied. Eighth-inch tempered bronzed glass is used in the doors.

inches (millimeters)

REFERENCE	QUANTITY	PART	STOCK	THICKNESS	(mm)	WIDTH	(mm)	LENGTH	(mm)	COMMENTS
A	4	legs	hardwood	1¾	(44)	1¾	(44)	59	(1499)	
B	1	top	hardwood	¾	(19)	14	(356)	48	(1219)	
C	2	top side rails	hardwood	¾	(19)	5	(127)	9½	(241)	
D	2	bottom side rails	hardwood	¾	(19)	8	(203)	9½	(241)	
E	4	side panels	plywood	¼	(6)	9⅜	(238)	33⅜	(848)	
F	1	front bottom apron	hardwood	¾	(19)	3¾	(95)	42	(1067)	
G	1	bottom	hardwood	¾	(19)	11	(279)	42¼	(1073)	
H	3	shelves	hardwood	¾	(19)	9½	(241)	42¼	(1073)	
I	1	back	plywood	¼	(6)	42	(1067)	44⅜	(1127)	
J	4	door stiles	hardwood	¾	(19)	2½	(63.5)	51¹³⁄₁₆	(1316)	
K	2	upper door rails	hardwood	¾	(19)	3½	(89)	16½	(419)	
L	2	lower door rails	hardwood	¾	(19)	5	(127)	16½	(419)	
M	2	door dividers	hardwood	¼	(6)	1	(25)	45¾	(1162)	
N	4	horizontal dividers	hardwood	¼	(6)	1	(25)	16¼	(413)	
O	8	door dividers	hardwood	¼	(6)	1	(25)	10⅜	(264)	
P	1	back top apron	hardwood	¾	(19)	5	(127)	42	(1067)	
Q	1	back bottom apron	hardwood	¾	(19)	8	(203)	42	(1067)	
R	1	bottom cleat	hardwood	¾	(19)	1	(25)	41	(1041)	
S	1	upper front cleat	hardwood	¾	(19)	3	(76)	43	(1092)	
T	4	short glass stops	hardwood	⅜	(9.5)	⅜	(9.5)	16	(406)	cut to fit
U	4	long glass stops	hardwood	⅜	(9.5)	⅜	(9.5)	44	(1118)	cut to fit
	2	tempered glass								
	6	door hinges								Woodcraft #130404
	2	door knobs								Woodcraft #130526
	2	knob back plates								Woodcraft #130521
	4	door adjustable catches								Woodcraft #27H39
	14	tabletop fasteners								Woodcraft #27N10
	12	shelf supports								Woodcraft #27I14

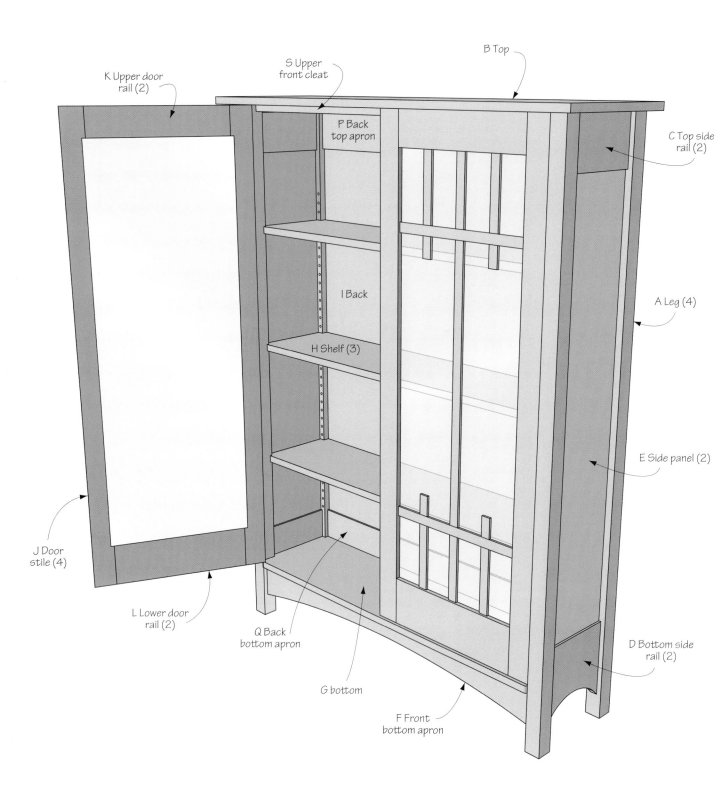

K Upper door rail (2)

S Upper front cleat

B Top

P Back top apron

C Top side rail (2)

I Back

A Leg (4)

H Shelf (3)

E Side panel (2)

J Door stile (4)

L Lower door rail (2)

Q Back bottom apron

D Bottom side rail (2)

G bottom

F Front bottom apron

1 Cut out the leg blanks. Then cut the long stopped grooves using a router table and a ¼"-diameter straight-cutting bit. Square the stopped ends using a chisel. Cut the mortises using a ½" Forstner drill bit and a chisel to square the mortises. Set up a drill press with a ¼" drill bit to drill the shelf-pin holes.

Make right and left front legs and left and right back legs. The back legs have two long grooves for the side and back panels. The front legs have only one long groove for the side panels.

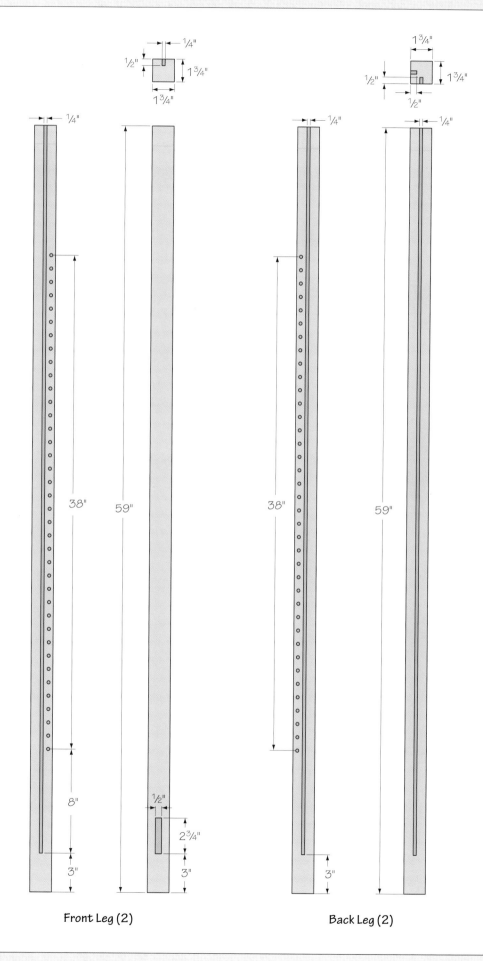

Front Leg (2)   Back Leg (2)

2 The top and bottom side rails involve several machining operations. Cut the tenons to fit the mortises in the legs. Cut the grooves for the side panels. Lay out the curves on the bottom aprons and cut them using a band saw or jigsaw. Cut the notches for the front top rail in the top side rails. Waste the bulk of the notch using a Forstner bit, the clean it up using a chisel.

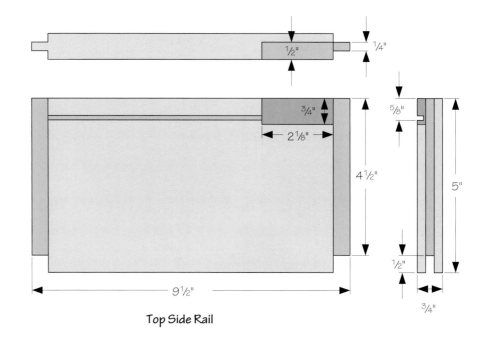

Top Side Rail

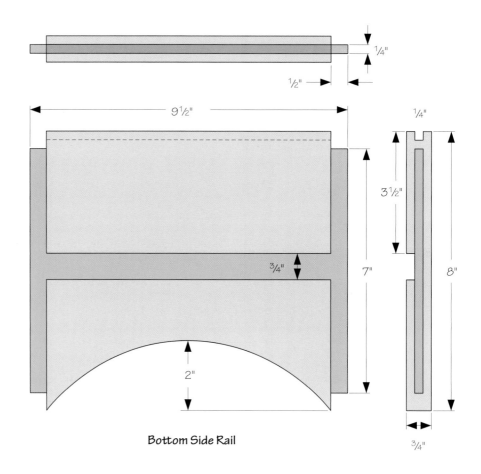

Bottom Side Rail

3 Cut the top front rail to size and cut the notches using a band saw. Cut the top back apron to size and cut the tenons to fit the long grooves in the legs. Cut the groove in the rail using a table saw. This groove will house the back panel. Then make a sawblade width cut for the tabletop fasteners. Lay out curve and cut it on the bottom rail using a band saw.

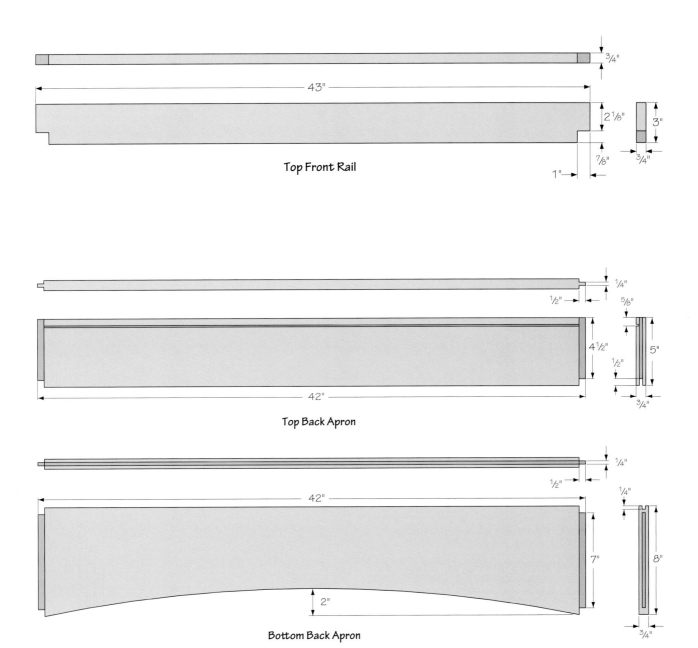

Top Front Rail

Top Back Apron

Bottom Back Apron

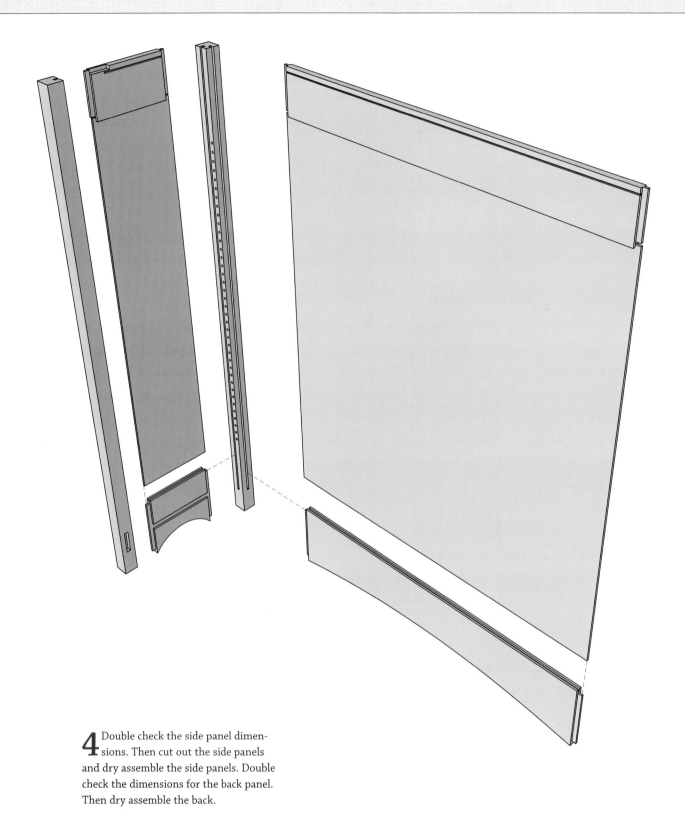

4 Double check the side panel dimensions. Then cut out the side panels and dry assemble the side panels. Double check the dimensions for the back panel. Then dry assemble the back.

5 Double check the dimensions for the bottom, then cut it to size and cut the notches using a band saw. Round the two outside front corners.

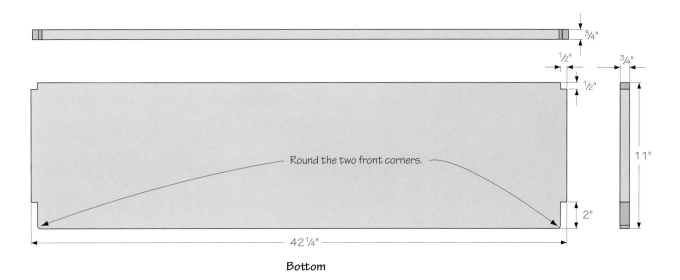

¾"

½" ¾"

½"

11"

Round the two front corners.

2"

42¼"

Bottom

6 Double check the dimensions for the shelves, then cut them to size and cut the notches using a band saw.

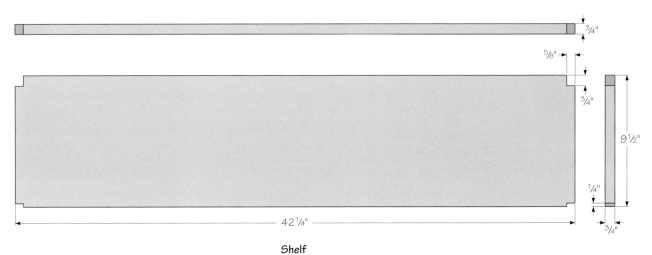

¾"

⅝"

¾"

9½"

¼"

42¼"

¾"

Shelf

7 Dry assemble the cabinet, including the top and bottom front rails and the bottom. If all the parts fit together well, disassemble and glue the cabinet together.

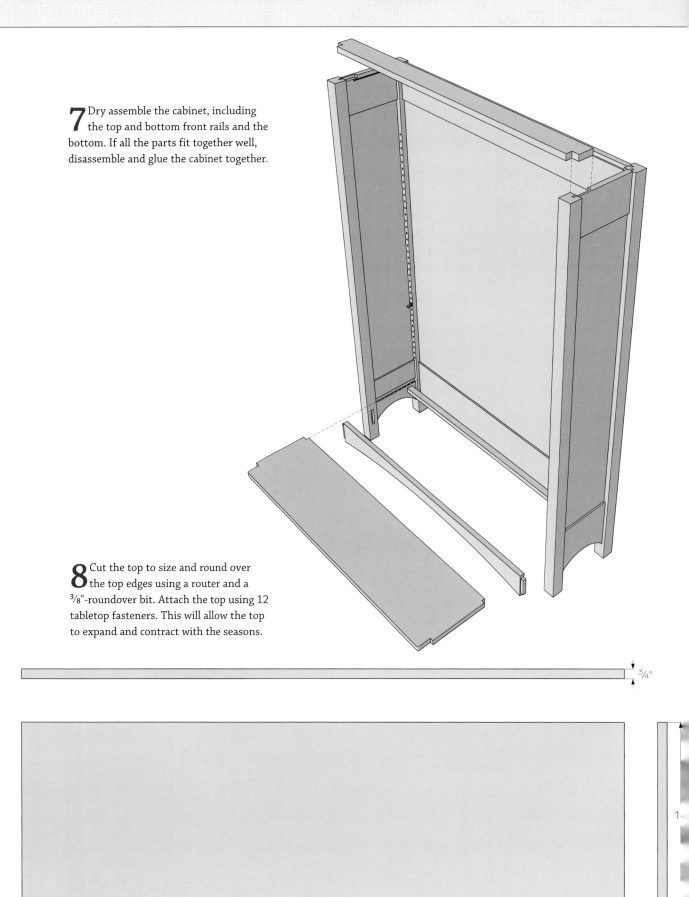

8 Cut the top to size and round over the top edges using a router and a ⅜"-roundover bit. Attach the top using 12 tabletop fasteners. This will allow the top to expand and contract with the seasons.

¾"

48"

¾"

1

Top

9 The door parts require some precision machining. Cut the stiles to dimension. Lay out the mortises and cut them as described in Step 1.

Cut the stopped rabbets using a router mounted in a router table. Square the corners using a chisel.

Cut the door dividers to size as per the cutting list. Now, lay out the notches for these dividers in the door stiles. Cut the notches to fit the door dividers.

Cut the top and bottom door rails to size and cut the tenons to fit the mortises in the door stiles. Cut the rabbets using the same setup you used for cutting the rabbets in the stiles. Finally, layout and cut the notches for the door dividers.

Take your time and lay out all the doorframe parts carefully. You will have two very attractive doors when you're done.

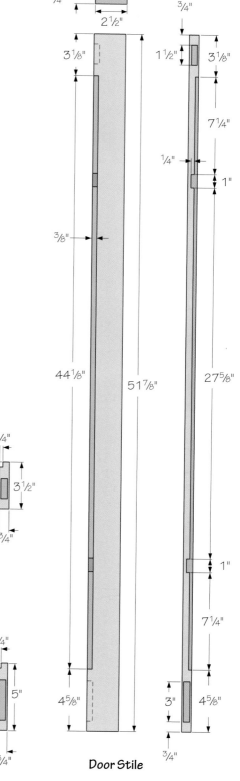

Upper Door Rail

Lower Door Rail

Door Stile

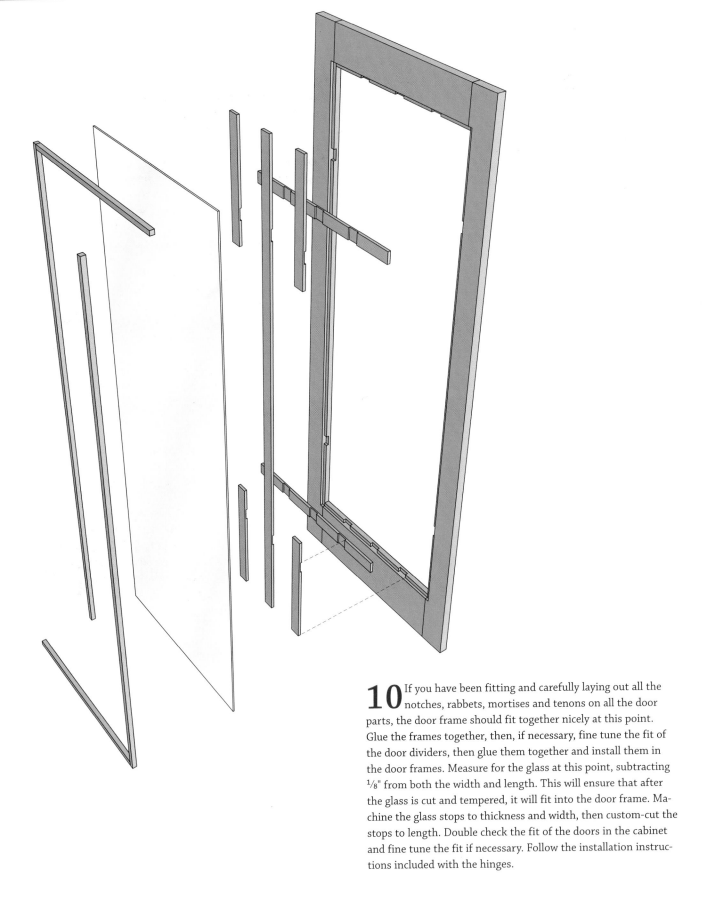

10 If you have been fitting and carefully laying out all the notches, rabbets, mortises and tenons on all the door parts, the door frame should fit together nicely at this point. Glue the frames together, then, if necessary, fine tune the fit of the door dividers, then glue them together and install them in the door frames. Measure for the glass at this point, subtracting $1/8$" from both the width and length. This will ensure that after the glass is cut and tempered, it will fit into the door frame. Machine the glass stops to thickness and width, then custom-cut the stops to length. Double check the fit of the doors in the cabinet and fine tune the fit if necessary. Follow the installation instructions included with the hinges.

METRIC CONVERSION CHART

to convert	to	multiply by
Inches	Centimeters	2.54
Centimeters	Inches	0.4
Feet	Centimeters	30.5
Centimeters	Feet	0.03
Yards	Meters	0.9
Meters	Yards	1.1

Distributed in Canada by Fraser Direct
100 Armstrong Avenue
Georgetown, Ontario L7G 5S4
Canada

Distributed in the U.K. and Europe by
F&W Media International, LTD
Brunel House, Forde Close
Newton Abbot
TQ12 4PU, UK
Tel: (+44) 1626 323200
Fax: (+44) 1626 323319
E-mail: enquiries@fwmedia.com

Distributed in Australia by Capricorn Link
P.O. Box 704
Windsor, NSW 2756
Australia

Visit our website at www.popularwoodworking.com or our consumer website at www.shopwoodworking.com for more woodworking information projects. Other fine Popular Woodworking Books are available from your local bookstore or direct from the publisher.

16 15 14 13 12   5 4 3 2 1

Acquisitions editor: David Thiel
Cover design: Geoff Raker
Interior design: Guy Kelly
Production coordinator: Mark Griffin
Editing & Illustrations: Jim Stack

fw media

Read This Import ant Safety Notice

To prevent accidents, keep safety in mind while you work. Use the safety guards installed on power equipment; they are for your protection. When working on power equipment, keep fingers away from saw blades, wear safety goggles to prevent injuries from flying wood chips and sawdust, wear hearing protection and consider installing a dust vacuum to reduce the amount of airborne sawdust in your woodshop.

Don't wear loose clothing, such as neckties or shirts with loose sleeves, or jewelry, such as rings, necklaces or bracelets, when working on power equipment. Tie back long hair to prevent it from getting caught in your equipment.

People who are sensitive to certain chemicals should check the chemical content of any product before using it. Due to the variability of local conditions, construction materials, skill levels, etc., neither the author nor Popular Woodworking Books assumes any responsibility for any accidents, injuries, damages or other losses incurred resulting from the material presented in this book.

The authors and editors who compiled this book have tried to make the contents as accurate and correct as possible. Plans, illustrations, photographs and text have been carefully checked. All instructions, plans and projects should be carefully read, studied and understood before beginning construction.

Prices listed for supplies and equipment were current at the time of publication and are subject to change.

ABOUT THE AUTHORS

Robert E. Belke, Sr. has been a custom furniture designer and builder for many years, working in the Shaker, Early American and Mission styles. He is the author of two previous books, ARTS & CRAFTS WOODWORKING PROJECTS and CLASSIC COUNTRY FURNITURE. Bob is a veteran of the United States Navy and worked for the General Electric Company in Syracuse, New York. Bob and his wife Carol have six grown children and live in Liverpool, New York.

Robert E. Belke, Jr. is a Technical Fellow and Manager at the Visteon Corporation. He is the holder of 43 patents in the U.S. and numerous foreign patents. He and his wife Rosemary currently reside in West Bloomfield, Michigan.

ACKNOWLEDGEMENTS

The authors would like to thank our wives, Carol, and the lovely Rosemary, for the encouragement they gave us. Additionally, our thanks go out to David Thiel, editor for Popular Woodworking Books, for all the excellent help he gave us during the publication process.

These and other great Popular Woodworking products are available at your local bookstore, woodworking store or online supplier.

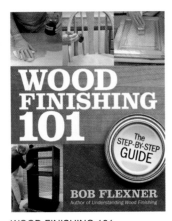

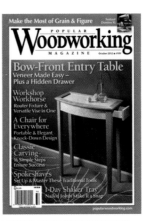

WOOD FINISHING 101
By Bob Flexner
Wood finishing doesn't have to be complicated or confusing. *Wood Finishing 101* boils it down to simple step-by-step instructions and pictures on how to finish common woods using widely available finishing materials. Bob Flexner has been writing about and teaching wood finishing for more than 20 years.

paperback • 128 pages

WEEKEND WOODWORKER'S PROJECT COLLECTION
This book has 40 projects from which to choose and, depending on the level of your woodworking skills, any of them can be completed in one or two weekends. Project s include: a game box, jewelry box, several styles of bookcases and shelves, mirrors, picture frames and more.

paperback • 256 pages

POPULAR WOODWORKING MAGAZINE
Whether learning a new hobby or perfecting your craft, *Popular Woodworking Magazine* provides seven issues a year with the expert information you need to learn the skills, not just build the project. Find the latest issue on newsstands, or you can order online at popularwoodworking.com.

SHOPCLASS VIDEOS
From drafting, to dovetails and even how to carve a ball-and-claw foot, our ShopClass Videos let you see the lesson as if you were standing right there.

Available at shopwoodworking.com
DVD & Instant download